W9-BHB-915

Compassionate
Capitalism

HOW
CORPORATIONS
CAN MAKE
DOING GOOD
AN INTEGRAL
PART OF
DOING WELL

MARC BENIOFF
&
KAREN SOUTHWICK

CAREER
PRESS
Franklin Lakes, NJ

Copyright © 2004 by Marc Benioff & Karen Southwick

All rights reserved under the Pan-American and International Copyright Conventions. This book may not be reproduced, in whole or in part, in any form or by any means electronic or mechanical, including photocopying, recording, or by any information storage and retrieval system now known or hereafter invented, without written permission from the publisher, The Career Press.

COMPASSIONATE CAPITALISM
EDITED BY CLAYTON W. LEADBETTER
TYPESET BY EILEEN DOW MUNSON
Cover design by Lu Rossman/Digi Dog Design
Printed in the U.S.A. by Book-mart Press

To order this title, please call toll-free 1-800-CAREER-1 (NJ and Canada: 201-848-0310) to order using VISA or MasterCard, or for further information on books from Career Press.

The Career Press, Inc., 3 Tice Road, PO Box 687,
Franklin Lakes, NJ 07417
www.careerpress.com

Library of Congress Cataloging-in-Publication Data

Benioff, Marc, 1969-
    Compassionate capitalism : how corporations can make doing good an integral part of doing well / by Marc Benioff & Karen Southwick.
        p. cm.
    Includes bibliographical references and index.
    ISBN 1-56414-714-2 (paper)
    1. Corporations—Charitable contributions—United States. 2. Social responsibility of business—United States. I. Title: Corporations can make doing good an integral part of doing business. II. Southwick, Karen. III. Title.

HG4028.C6B46 2004
658.15'3--dc22

                                                                    2003065358

This book is dedicated to
all past, present, and future corporate leaders
who strive to use
the resources of their companies
to make the world a better place,
and to the next generation of entrepreneurs
who will see the power of
the integrated philanthropy model
and how it can make
a positive impact on society.

Acknowledgments

We would especially like to commend the untiring efforts of Suzanne DiBianca, head of the salesforce.com Foundation, in providing information, support, and encouragement in making this book happen, while, at the same time, overseeing the company's philanthropic endeavors. In addition, we would like to thank all those companies, nonprofit organizations, and other experts who gave of their time and energy to do interviews. Without them and their examples of "best practices," there could be no book of this sort. Finally, we thank Career Press and its editors for having the heart to publish this book and the brains to make it successful.

Contents

Foreword
By Alan Hassenfeld,
Chairman, Hasbro, Inc.

As the former CEO and now chairman of Hasbro, I have learned from family heritage how important it is to give back to the communities where you work and live. Hasbro has been a family-run organization since inception. My grandfather and his two brothers started the company in 1923. Then my father and his brother ran it, then my brother and myself, and finally myself. We believe in living charity in my family, where we get out and participate personally, and we've tried to pass on that commitment to our company. Twenty years ago, we started the Hasbro Charitable Trust to provide support to the communities where we operate and to manage our product donation programs. Eighteen years ago, we also established the Hasbro Children's Foundation to provide funding nationwide for difficult issues affecting children from birth to age 12. We've concentrated on kids, because that's the source of our success as a company. We feel as though we have to be a resource for solving some of the problems that confront children and their families today.

So I am especially pleased to introduce this book that describes the "best practices" in corporate philanthropy, by companies small and large, including salesforce.com and Hasbro. When Marc Benioff was starting salesforce.com, he asked me to sit on the board. He also asked my advice on inculcating a culture of service within the overall business goals of salesforce.com. I told him one thing you need to do is start early, so that employees, customers, investors, and others realize that this is an important priority. There is nothing wrong with fitting your philanthropic goals closely with the goals of the business. It can be a win-win for everyone that way. Another thing you must do is make the philanthropic program matter to your employees, get them involved in the community. It is good for business and good for employee morale and loyalty. Here at Hasbro, we believe in the motto "you make a living by what you do, you make a life by what you give." I believe that community service programs of the kind you will see in this book allow executives and employees to make a balanced life by giving.

Some observers suggest that a corporation's primary business is business. That is, we should not devote time and resources to issues that distract us from the bottom line. But I would submit that we cannot have a strong bottom line without having strong communities around us. For it is from our communities that we draw our employees, our customers, our supporters, and our critics. Without vibrant, active communities, we lose our own vitality. The last few years, which have seen many companies, including my own, go through difficult times, have underscored the relationship between businesses and the communities in which they reside. When the communities are suffering, so are we. At Hasbro, we recognize that connection, and so, even when we were struggling through losses, layoffs, and restructuring, our philanthropic programs still survived. While the actual dollars available for grants decreased, other programs took their place—such as a volunteer program that allowed employees to take four hours a month paid time off to work with children. Community is part of our mission statement, and you don't abandon your mission statement just because times are tough.

You'll learn from this compelling book, coauthored by Marc and veteran journalist Karen Southwick, how important philanthropy is and what kind of positive messages it sends to your employees and to outside stakeholders. You'll discover how some of the best practitioners of good community service—among them IBM, Timberland, Hewlett-Packard, LensCrafters, Wells Fargo, and many others—have put their ideals into practice. The examples of salesforce.com and smaller companies included in the book will demonstrate that giving back is not a matter of size nor of longevity, but of early and sustained commitment.

That commitment must come from the executives of the company, particularly the CEO, and extend down to the newest employee. It must be reinforced at company meetings and integrated within the corporation. I'll put it bluntly: We want to get companies that don't give to start giving. People can't take it with them. Salesforce.com is a wonderful model, because, starting at the top, Marc has the passion. If you have passion and let your people become involved, the sky's the limit on what the company can do.

Indeed, in the wake of the recent scandals that have tarnished corporate America, I would urge all companies to reexamine their relationships with their communities and determine how they can do a better job of becoming socially responsible entities. Integral to doing a better job is getting out and knowing your community through service. It is essential that you see the community's priorities and needs through working side-by-side with nonprofits and government agencies charged with meeting those needs. Community service, as a key component of the broader concept of social responsibility, keeps us connected to the larger world and keeps us grounded in our humanity. But community service cannot be performed well within a silo. It should not be shunted off into a single department or relegated to a single manager. It should be a living, breathing part of every company's culture and mission, alongside profitability, innovation, and good business practices.

If a company wants to be part of the 21st century, it must understand and value community service. And then the company must put all of its resources—including donations of money and equipment, employee time, and corporate expertise—into that mission. This will not come at the expense of business goals, but it will augment them. If your stakeholders see you as not only a good place to do business, but also as a *good* member of the community, they are more likely to buy from you and to want to be associated with you. Many consumers today are making purchase decisions based on corporate reputation. Shareholders are behaving similarly in their investment choices. I believe that the competitive advantage you gain from being a caring and sharing company is significant; it instills in your people a higher integrity level. In turn, stakeholders want to be associated with a company that has a heart. Community service: You do it because it's the right thing to do, but it's also the profitable thing to do.

Introduction

Dare to Be Great

Everyone is great because everyone can serve.
—Martin Luther King, Jr.

Shortly after Jim Steele became president of salesforce.com in late 2002, he got to go on a field trip. Along with several employees, Steele went to an elementary school in San Francisco's Chinatown district, where salesforce.com has funded a computer center for the students. Employees volunteer time there on a regular basis to teach the kids about computers, work on spelling and grammar, set up a word-processing document, and get plugged into the Internet. Steele figured he'd be an observer, watching the employees do the mentoring. Fat chance. Right after he walked in the door, a young girl grabbed his hand. "Are you the boss?" she asked him, with that intuition that children sometimes have. "I want you to make sure all my words are spelled correctly." Those kids, recalls Steele, brought the notion of serving the community "to real life for me." His previous company, a start-up like salesforce.com, had not made philanthropy a priority. Salesforce.com has done so from the beginning, deeming community service as important as any core competency on the business side. "Until you actually get out there and do it yourself, you don't appreciate it," says Steele. "I walk into this school and meet these excited, smart little kids interested in business and technology. And they all know salesforce.com."

Jeff Swartz, CEO of the Timberland Company, had a similar experience. About 15 years ago, when he was chief operating officer of the apparel company, he donated 50 pairs of boots in response to a letter from a fledgling nonprofit organization called City Year. The letter referred to the youthful executive as a "tycoon," artfully flattering his ego. He sent off the boots, figured he'd get a thank-you note, and that would be the end of it. Not quite. Instead of a letter, one of the cofounders of City Year showed up on his doorstep. He told Swartz, "My job is to redeem the community. I can show you how to combine your job and mine. Give me four hours." Swartz bit. He, a group of employees, and five City Year members spent half a day working with troubled youth at a drug rehabilitation center in Stratham, New Hampshire, where Timberland is headquartered. At the end of the day, one of the volunteers from Timberland, a middle-aged woman, came up to Swartz with tears in her eyes. "Thank you for letting me serve here," she told him. "Six years ago my child went through this program." Swartz had a shiver of epiphany: *How much clearer does it have to be,* he thought, *that this drug rehab center is our community as much as the hallways of Timberland? This is our opportunity to exert leadership and share strength.* "It was like an icy shower on a cold morning," recalls Swartz. "My heart was pounding and my senses were tingling. It was better than Disney World, better even than watching the Red Sox beat the Yankees. It wasn't the power of title; it was the power of transformation." City Year had introduced him to the power of community service and shown him that "this was possible and accessible in a 15-minute drive down the street in our own community." Today, Timberland is City Year's biggest corporate partner, and the two have immeasurably enriched each other in ways that have nothing to do with money.

Both salesforce.com and Timberland are companies where integrated philanthropy is practiced. Although they do generously fund nonprofit endeavors, their philanthropy is not merely a matter of writing a check and volunteering for a day or two. The spirit of community service permeates both companies on many levels. Employees and executives alike get involved, on their own and through events coordinated by the companies in partnership with nonprofit agencies. The corporate giving organization isn't a silo, as it is in many companies, set up primarily to wring some good public relations from handing over checks to various agencies that are then quickly forgotten. Service is a core part of the culture and operations that enables these companies to prosper. At salesforce.com, we call this the "integrated model of philanthropy," in which we dedicate employee time and portions of our equity and profits to helping the communities where we're located. The salesforce.com Foundation, established very early in the young company's history, is headed by Suzanne DiBianca, a former management consultant who caught the vision of community service and wanted to transition to this kind of work. About six months after the company's launch, DiBianca joined salesforce.com. "I was really excited about what salesforce.com was doing," she says. "This was my chance to pioneer a new model that was built for the long haul. I saw the power that community service could have on a company as part of its long-term culture." Steele saw that too; it was part of what drew him to salesforce.com. "This is the first company I'd seen in a while grounded in deep-rooted values from day one," he says. "As we're successful, we share it with the community." Steele says he could go back and explain to his family, "Look what I'm doing," and be proud of it.

In the early days of industrial America, when many companies were family-owned, philanthropy seemed to be a natural component of the corporate mission. The people who ran the company had grown up in the community and wanted to give back to those whom they recognized as friends and neighbors. Then, as corporations grew larger, ownership shifted away from family management and that sense of obligation to the community grew dimmer. The senior executives hadn't necessarily grown up in the headquarters community and, besides, companies had expanded to multiple sites, domestically and overseas. What was community anymore? Sadly, many companies today appear to embrace economist Milton Friedman's notion that "the one and only business of business is maximizing profit, playing within the rules of the game." But in this era of globalization, where corporations are often targets of protest for the changes they bring to communities worldwide, giving back becomes more important to demonstrate unity and understanding. Besides, no company can expect long-term success with the community languishing. If there's anything that the current economic downturn shows us, it's that the prosperity of business is dependent upon the prosperity of the United States, indeed the world, as a whole.

Dick Kovacevich, the CEO of Wells Fargo & Co., puts it forcefully: "There are too many free loaders, businesses that benefit from quality of life in the community but don't participate in that quality." He singles out Silicon Valley, which perhaps more than any other region has enjoyed boom times and struggled through busts. "It's a shame to see the lack of [philanthropic] contributions from Silicon Valley, versus the amount of money being made there," he says. Kovacevich, whose own company is a leading corporate donor in the San Francisco Bay Area and elsewhere, says he has seen the increased needs on the part of nonprofits and the people they serve. That means there are "increased needs for companies to give proportionately," he says. "We're not doing a very good job in the business community. We need to tap companies that are not giving today. Unless we can do that, I'm not optimistic about the nonprofits' abilities to serve the needs of their communities." He adds that doing philanthropy does not conflict with a for-profit mission but rather enhances it. "When you do these things it will help your bottom line," he says. "The family [business] owners knew that instinctively." Levi Strauss & Co. CEO Phil Marineau agrees with him. Those who have been successful in business "were lucky enough to have had a support system and to get an education," he says. "None of us completely deserves what we've got. When we work at a home-less shelter, we see that there, but for the grace of God, go I."

Some companies today, entrepreneurial start-ups in particular, seem inclined to wait until they get bigger to establish a philanthropic effort. The problem with that is it doesn't make community service a part of the culture, and changing a corporate culture is always difficult. Says Steele, "If you wait until you get big, you'll never do it right. It has to be built into the culture from day one. It's either part of you or it's not. If it's not, you're going to make a half-assed effort." That takes leadership from the top, as executives like Swartz, Kovacevich, Marineau, and others have shown. Momentum builds when leaders champion the cause of com-munity service, incorporating it within everyday activities and trumpeting it in companywide meetings. Timberland, for example, designates a day of service as a regular part of its sales meetings. Salesforce.com includes service projects in employee orientation sessions, and foundation head DiBianca addresses company meetings along with the other top execu-tives. Wells Fargo directs its bank branch managers to go out into their respective communities and find a nonprofit agency to help.

Other companies have cut back on their philanthropy amid a challenging economy, reasoning that they can restore it when times get better. But that approach ignores the fact that the needs of the community are greater than ever, and that reducing help sends a troubling signal to employees, shareholders, and others. Mike McLaughlin, a partner with Deloitte Consulting, speaks for many when he says, "It's more important today than ever before to do philanthropy. Even though we in the corporate world are having our own business challenges, we have to find ways to help." When philanthropy is integrated within the corporate mission, it's easier to find ways to help and more difficult to stop helping when times are tough. "Great companies and business leaders of the past looked for social needs in defining their business," notes Bill Shireman, CEO of the Global Futures Foundation. "The social need offered a strategic advantage to the company that perceived it." For example, in the early 20th century, Henry Ford saw that the growing middle class craved mobility in the form of reliable, relatively cheap, individualized transportation, and he delivered it. Likewise, Citigroup has a program where it allows people to open very small cash deposits to invest in stocks and investment vehicles. "Put the two together and poorer people can invest and save for the first time," says Shireman. Although these are not philanthropic programs per se, they grow out of involvement with community.

The model of philanthropy that we're proposing in this book sees business and community needs as closely aligned and encourages companies to make serving the community a central focus. The model of philanthropy as a separate, negligible afterthought is washed up. The new model says that philanthropy must be woven into every thread of corporate existence so that it becomes a part of the cultural fabric and cannot be pulled out without pulling apart the corporation itself. Organizations that have service as a core value of their culture will see both intrinsic and external returns. All people desire to have their lives make a difference, so the segmentation of work life and service life is not only outdated but also detrimental to the effective functioning of an organization. It is simply part of being human to be able to give, and companies that provide the opportunity will find that it energizes employees and executives. Once begun, a philanthropic mission takes on a life of its own—not a burden, but a joy.

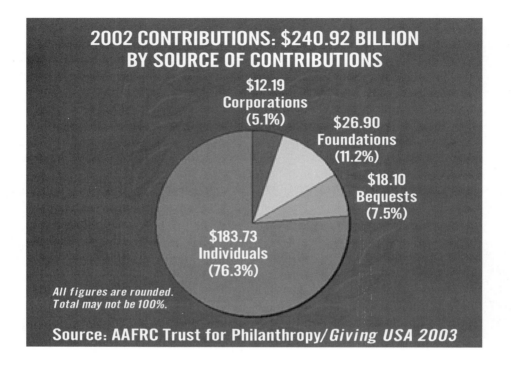

2002 CONTRIBUTIONS: $240.92 BILLION
BY SOURCE OF CONTRIBUTIONS

$12.19
Corporations
(5.1%)

$26.90
Foundations
(11.2%)

$18.10
Bequests
(7.5%)

$183.73
Individuals
(76.3%)

All figures are rounded.
Total may not be 100%.

Source: AAFRC Trust for Philanthropy/*Giving USA 2003*

Corporate giving has historically represented only a small part (around 5 percent) of cash and in-kind contributions within the United States, so there's plenty of room to do more. Individuals, bequests, and family and private foundations represent the bulk of giving. However, in recent years, the growth rate in corporate giving has outstripped that of other donors. According to Giving USA, an annual report of charitable donations in the United States released by the American Association of Fund-Raising Consul (AAFRC) Trust for Philanthropy, corporate giving jumped 10.5 percent to $12.2 billion in 2002, compared to $11 billion the previous year. (That figure includes cash and in-kind donations.) By contrast, total donations of $240.9 billion—which also included giving by individuals, bequests, and foundations—increased only 1 percent from the previous year. The AAFRC report, which was researched by the Center on Philanthropy at Indiana University, attributed the increase in corporate giving to several factors, including an increase in corporate foundation grantmaking, continued fulfillment of pledges made in 2001, and growth of in-kind giving such as donations of computers or other equipment. The 10.5-percent increase—which occurred in a difficult climate for companies—shows that corporate giving is the growth area for philanthropy.

But it's not just a matter of money. Businesses have much to contribute beyond dollars and equipment; they have their expertise, their leverage, and the enthusiasm of their employees. Corporations can be "the most powerful player in the nonprofit sector and philanthropy," asserts Mark Kramer, managing director of the Foundation Strategy Group. "By using all of their resources, they can do more than private foundations, individual donors, and community foundations." What this book intends to do is to show companies large and small how they can use all of their resources to help their communities and, in doing so, help themselves and their employees as well. We could double that 5 percent easily within a year if all companies recognized service as a part of their mission. In this book, we'll demonstrate that there's no need to wait to be philanthropic by showing you very small, as well as very large, companies that have incorporated service successfully and reaped myriad benefits for themselves and the community. In the chapters ahead, we will explain how to establish a culture of philanthropy, define a mission, involve employees, sustain philanthropy in good times and bad, expand it globally, measure its impact, and forge strong partnerships with nonprofits. We will show you, using real-life examples from dozens of corporations and nonprofits, how you can dare to be great by integrating community service within your company.

Establishing a Culture of Philanthropy

Suzanne DiBianca, executive director of the salesforce.com Foundation, was escorting a journalist writing a piece on the company around the office. DiBianca offered her usual boast that "anybody here in this office can tell you what the foundation does." The journalist retorted (as journalists are apt to do), "Prove it." So DiBianca and the journalist stopped at the cubicles of random employees and asked about the foundation's mission. "We got consistent answers all the way to the door," recalls DiBianca. The foundation carries out salesforce.com's vision, which is to offer integrated philanthropy within both local and global communities where the company has a presence. Middle-school and high-school students who attend technology training programs offered by the foundation have the same privilege as the journalist. "I will take the kids on a tour, stop at a new employee's desk, and ask them to explain the foundation's mission," says DiBianca. "It is one of the primary drivers of our culture. We test that all the time."

Indeed, the first criterion for doing philanthropy well is making it part of the corporate culture. This may seem obvious in theory, but it is not obvious in practice. As the economy worsened in the early years of the new millennium, many companies were forced to concentrate on their very survival. Philanthropy often seemed to take a back seat to issues such as layoffs, salary cuts, pressure for increased productivity, executive compensation, and other contentious matters. If you're worried about keeping your job and paying your bills, do you care whether your company is donating to the homeless shelter down the street or matching your contribution to the American Cancer Society? If it's become a part of the company culture—and your own internal motivation—yes, you do. "I'm a sales contributor working 10–12 hours a day. If I have some time off helping at Raphael House [a homeless shelter] or somewhere else, it puts a human face on a very aggressive environment," says Bryan Breckenridge, a sales account executive at salesforce.com. If he ever goes to another company, he will look for one that places a high priority on philanthropy. "It's too important to me now not to do it," he says.

So the question becomes, how do you establish a culture of philanthropy? As with any company cultural issue, leadership must come from the top. The CEO must make philanthropy a centerpiece of the company's mission, just like manufacturing a great product or earning profits or giving shareholders a good return. But it must be more than lip service or devotion to giving as a way to generate PR coverage. The CEO himself or herself must demonstrate a commitment to philanthropy in bad times and good by establishing policies and processes that foster corporate service, such as employee time off for charitable work, recognition of employees who do such work, matching gifts, and other incentives. "Our job should be to take service and the notions of commerce and justice and link them together," says Jeffrey Swartz, CEO of the Timberland Company. "I want this notion to be so well developed that, if we hire some outsider to come in here and run this company, she wouldn't think twice that this is a service organization. I want it to be immutable." The CEO's attitude must permeate the company; in particular, middle managers must recognize that allowing employees reasonable amounts of time off to perform community service is not a loss to them, but a gain in overall productivity and balance. Finally, employees have to be convinced that senior management is truly dedicated to the notion of philanthropy and will not somehow penalize those who don't spend every waking hour either working or thinking about the company's products and marketing.

Numerous companies have done great jobs in creating a culture of giving. Here, we pick out four as examples: two older companies, Hasbro and Timberland, and two relatively new ones, Cisco and salesforce.com. Although the quartet has taken, for the most part, different approaches to how they do community service, they've all succeeded in making it a basic building block of their cultures.

Hasbro, Inc.

Hasbro, maker of famous toys and games such as Mr. Potato Head, Tonka trucks, Monopoly, and Scrabble, doesn't play around when it comes to philanthropy. Chairman Alan Hassenfeld, who stepped down as CEO in mid-2003, is the third generation of his family to lead the 80-year-old company. Hassenfeld's grandfather and two brothers emigrated to the United States from a village on the Russian-Polish border and founded the company in 1923. "They managed to bring a lot of people over here from that village, Ulanov, which was destroyed during the war," says Hassenfeld. "I grew up in a home that absolutely believed in giving back." When Hassenfeld's father died in 1979, he left a note for his wife and three children. "I haven't left anything to charity," it said. "I leave it to you in different trusts. I have taught you all well, and I believe in living charity." The note went on to talk about the elder Hassenfeld's conviction that his children would also want to make a difference, so he wasn't going to tie their hands by specifying where to use the money. "I'd rather you take what you've learned and be able to make a difference in your own time."

As chairman, Hassenfeld continues to lead the company's philanthropic endeavors. "I have this awful expression, 'the fish rots from the head,'" he says. "If the CEO/Chairman believes in giving back and making a difference, that becomes one of the cornerstones of a company. If he doesn't, then it's lacking." But Hassenfeld agrees the leader also has to walk the walk. "It's one thing to talk about it; it's another to try to get your people involved and empowered." To that end, Hasbro allows employees four hours a month of paid time off to do community service. When it hires in senior managers, "we look at what they've done" in areas outside business, says Hassenfeld. "Has their own concern been only for profits, or has there been a sense of caring?"

Hasbro's primary philanthropic mission, both through its charitable trust and foundation, is to make the world a better place for children. "It's always been kids, because that's where our success as a company has come from," says Hassenfeld. "This is our payback. We're so close to the needs and plight of children that we have to be a force in improving their world." In 18 years of giving, the Hasbro Children's Foundation has awarded more than $40 million in grants to agencies benefiting disadvantaged families and helped more than a million young children. Employees have also racked up thousands of hours volunteering at agencies and helping to build playgrounds and other facilities.

Hassenfeld, who serves on 14 nonprofit boards, remembers visiting the Hasbro Children's Hospital in Providence, Rhode Island, that opened in 1992. "I had dreamed of a hospital where no child would die, but of course it doesn't work that way," he says. When they broke ground on the hospital, he walked around the site with a young boy on chemotherapy, talking about the hospital that might make a difference in his life and other children's. Every year at Christmas, Hassenfeld, other senior managers, and their spouses go room to room, giving out toys and cookies to the kids at the hospital and talking to their families. "We spend about four or five hours at the hospital. We literally are trying to bring smiles," he says. Making the rounds of the hospital "puts me back in my place." Someone at the top of a company sees the world from very high levels. "This brings me back to earth and says, 'make sure the company can do this, because this makes a difference in people's lives.'"

Another project with which Hasbro is involved is Operation Smile, in which poor children with cleft palates get needed surgery. When Operation Smile personnel made a presentation to Hasbro employees, showing before-and-after pictures, "it made you realize what some families go through just to get what is here a simple and fairly inexpensive operation," says Hassenfeld. He also joined employees when they built a Boundless Playground in Rhode Island, which adapts playground equipment such as swings and slides to disabled children. One Hasbro employee had a 14-year-old daughter who was confined to a wheelchair and had never been on a swing. When they finished the work and dedicated the playground, the girl was able to use a swing for the first time. "Her mom hugged me and said, 'This is one of the finest days of my life, not only for me, but for what we've done for people with different handicaps.'" Sums up Hassenfeld: "That's the payoff."

Even though Hasbro has had to cut its philanthropic budget in diffi-cult economic times, Hassenfeld picks up the slack out of his family foundation. "I haven't cut back," he says. "We've reached more kids because we have really pushed the grantee organizations harder than ever [to use the funds effectively and get matching grants]. Our job is to make sure that every penny is working hard." And so, even in tough times, employees such as the mother of the 14-year-old "will say they're proud to be part of this company because we believe in trying to make the communities we live in a better place."

The Timberland Company

Timberland has a lot in common with Hasbro. Both companies are based in New England, with strong corporate responsibility ethics. Both are also headed by the third generation of the original founders. In Timberland's case, that's Jeffrey Swartz, whose grandfather Nathan launched the predecessor company in 1952. Swartz started with the com-pany in 1986, worked in virtually every functional area, and became presi-dent and CEO in 1998. Under his leadership, Timberland, which makes footwear and apparel for outdoor activities, has expanded globally, reach-ing $1.2 billion in sales in 2002. In that same year, the company received the Ron Brown Award, which recognizes outstanding corporate lead-ership in social responsibility. "Timberland is on this earth to make superior boots, shoes, clothing, and accessories—but that's not all we can do," says Swartz. "We create value for our four groups of constituents: employees, consumers, shareholders, and the community. Everything we do at Timberland should derive from our values." That belief in doing good and doing well has led to a 15-year partnership with City Year, a nationwide youth service initiative that aims to improve the urban environment.

"Our mission is to equip people to make a difference in the world," explains Carolyn Casey, director of social enterprise for Timberland. "Commitment to service is in the DNA of the company. We have four values: humanity, humility, integrity, and excellence." She adds that Timberland employees aren't expected to be automatons interested solely in the corporate's for-profit efforts. "We like to celebrate the fact that when you, as an employee, walk into Timberland, you don't have to check the rest of yourself at the door," she says. "You're still a whole self, a mother or grandfather. We value that service part of your life and what you bring to the job." Adds Swartz, "If we are about equipping people to make a difference in the world, it should be relevant to us that kids can't get an education in the public schools."

Exemplifying that, when Timberland sends its salespeople or its executives off to a meeting, the extracurricular activities aren't big bashes or trips around the countryside. They're service projects and, says Casey, "No one's there for show. They're working hard." For example, at a sales meeting in Park City, Utah, in December 2002, about 200 salespeople took a day to do community service. There were 60 people who helped build affordable housing in Park City, which is known primarily for its upscale ski resort. Another 30 people worked at the Peace House, a home for victims of domestic violence. "Our final thing—one of the most inspirational—was working with migrant families who work at the resort," recalls Casey. Many of the children didn't have proper outerwear for the winter cold in Utah. "We identified about 70 children and partnered each of them with a Timberland buddy," she says. "We outfitted these kids from head to toe, and they spent the day with their buddy," playing games, having lunch. In the afternoon, the children, most of whom had never skiied, got a free lesson donated by the resort. In the evening, a Timberland sales executive performed a magic show. "It was just a breathtaking day," Casey says. In addition to the direct service, Timberland also made grants to several organizations in the region to combat hunger. Swartz and another executive spoke at a local high school about the importance of including service in the corporate mission. The CEO also addressed the local Rotary Club about Timberland's commitment to community.

Swartz says the most meaningful day for him, personally, came on September 11, 2002, a year after the 9/11 tragedy, when his son accompanied him on a Timberland service day. The year before, on September 11, 2001, Swartz was with 150 other Timberland executives and employees performing a day of service at an inner-city school in the Bronx. "I remember coming out of that [New York] hotel and seeing the smoke in the sky," he recalls. Swartz and the others decided to continue with their service. "We got on the bus and went to the Bronx," to build a playground and computer room at the school. The following year, on the same day, "we went back there to do more service," says Swartz. His then 12-year-old son, Sam, had told his father, "I want to serve with you." Swartz adds, "That was a day of transformation I cannot describe. It was the creation of a bond with Sam, who's looking forward to September 11, 2003."

It was the serendipitous partnership with City Year that prompted Timberland's formal commitment to philanthropy, although the company had already been making cash and product donations in a smaller way to various organizations. (See Chapter 12 for more on national partnerships.) Swartz, who absorbed the service ethic through his family, developed a passionate attachment to City Year's mission that led to a deep partnership with far-flung impact. City Year New Hampshire is housed at Timberland; the company outfits teams of young people and sends employees to work side by side with them in numerous locations. Swartz served as chairman of City Year and helped instill business practices that enabled it to expand nationwide. It all started in 1989 when City Year, which was just getting started and described itself as an urban peace corps, wrote Timberland and asked for a donation of boots for the young people it was enlisting. Swartz, then the COO, responded personally and sent the boots. He and other Timberland managers went out and served with the program. Says Casey, "That day really sparked in him this desire to see a formalized service program." In addition to doing projects with City Year, Swartz launched a Path of Service program in which employees get paid time off to give back to the community. Path of Service also incorporates the service days during such events as the sales meeting in Park City. Other locations for these types of events have extended from Prague, where employees from more than 20 countries united to help that city recover from a devastating flood, to Pasadena, where a Timberland team spent a day at a local school. Employees can also apply for up to six months of full-time, paid leave to work at a nonprofit. "Someone from our sales team is currently working at an orphanage in Peru," Casey says.

As she sums up, even in difficult times, such as the mid-1990s, when Timberland had to do its first layoffs ever, "We have never pulled back from our commitment to the community. At Timberland it isn't an either-or. It's part of us." Swartz says he wouldn't have considered backing away from service. "I've heard all those criticisms that it should only be about business," he says, "but the core of what we stand for is values and actions. If we don't animate the mission and live the values, I don't know what else we're doing here." In the mid-1990s, when Timberland was struggling, "we doubled the amount of hours we served," he says. "It would have been as logical to say to Timberland people you've got to come to work without your clothes on as to say we're back to a pure commerce model. They would have been aghast." Swartz says Timberland's turnaround and its business success—as demonstrated by such measures as the highest return on investment capital in its space and highest percentage of revenues from new products—derive from "the strength of our community."

Cisco Systems, Inc.

Cisco was one of those wild success stories for which Silicon Valley is justifiably famous, up until a few years ago when the technology market crashed and burned. In 1984, a husband and wife team, Leonard Bosack and Sandy Lerner, attending Stanford University, figured out how to connect computer networks by using a router, which directs pieces of information to their various destinations via a centralized network. They got venture capital funding and started a company. From this beginning sprang a powerhouse that, a mere 15 years after its founding, had become one of the three most valuable companies on the planet, along with General Electric and Microsoft. In the general upheaval of the technology market, Cisco tumbled from that lofty perch, but it is still considered one of the most important players in the technology revolution. At the same time, it has earned a reputation for doing innovative philanthropy, which included paying laid-off employees (who got into the Cisco Fellowship program) a third of their usual salaries, with full benefits, to go work in the nonprofit world for a year. (For more on maintaining philanthropy in bad times, see Chapter 6.) Peter Tavernise, now executive director of the Cisco Foundation, is one of those laid-off employees. After he lost his job at a North Carolina Cisco office in April 2001, Tavernise became a Cisco Fellow, spending a year doing fund-raising and strategic planning for a nonprofit in Durham. He then rejoined Cisco as an employee and took the reins of the foundation, established in 1998 with a stock endowment.

Even before the foundation was organized, Cisco had a history of giving back. Lerner, who departed the company in 1990 with $200 million in stock, set the example. Cisco's original headquarters adjoined an elementary school in impoverished East Palo Alto, and "we had employees jumping the fence to go mentor students and buy equipment for the school," says Tavernise, all with Lerner's encouragement and financial support. After John Morgridge, a technology industry veteran, joined Cisco in 1988 as president and CEO, he instilled a couple of core values that remain: frugality and giving back to the community. The CEO, who insisted that every employee, including himself, fly coach on business trips, was also personally matching employees' gifts to local food banks.

As it has grown into a major international company under the leadership of John Chambers, who took over from Morgridge in 1995, Cisco's philanthropic mission has evolved into building strong global communities by addressing such needs as hunger and education. In keeping with its entrepreneurial culture, Cisco allows employees to drive some of the philanthropy by selecting nonprofits in which they are interested. "We match their giving with dollars and with volunteerism," says Tavernise. "A lot of our philanthropy has grown up following our employees." For example, one overseas office sent volunteer employee labor to build nine houses in Guatemala and sponsored 100 more with matching funding from the corporation.

Because of its prowess in networking, Cisco often gives equipment to help nonprofits harness technology more effectively. Employees also give a lot of volunteer time to technology and other efforts—in 2002 the total was 38,170 hours. The Cisco Fellowship program, installed to give employees such as Tavernise a bridge when the company had to do serious layoffs in the early 2000s, has morphed into the Leadership Development Program. This involves selecting interested Cisco employees to work on-site at a nonprofit. For example, three employees spent a year and a half at the Second Harvest Food Bank, serving two Silicon Valley counties, with 150 locations. Cisco donated barcode scanning technology, which was installed by its employees who then trained food bank workers. That technology let the Food Bank put referrals into a database instead of a card catalog, and saved the equivalent of about 2 million meals a year, Tavernise says. Now that expertise is being transferred to other

29

communities where Cisco resides, such as North Carolina. Employees who work at the nonprofits develop skills in managing projects and exerting leadership of diverse groups that are transferable back to the corporation. "Productivity is the byword at the company and at our work with nonprofits," says Tavernise.

Salesforce.com

At salesforce.com, several members of the executive team came from Oracle Corporation, where we learned the hard way that waiting too long to develop a philanthropic culture really doesn't work. When I was an executive at Oracle in 1997, CEO Larry Ellison came to me, gave me a $100-million budget, and told me to go do philanthropy. While Oracle's funding—$10 million over 10 years to get computers into schools—undoubtedly did some good, I wasn't able to call on Oracle resources or employees to the extent I would have liked, because it was not part of the culture. They were unaware. So, when I founded salesforce.com, based in San Francisco, in late 1999, I decided to start the philanthropic model at the same time. I wanted to do an integrated model from day one. Our dream is to have a company whose core value is service—that is able not only to deliver market share and return but to serve the communities we're in. To that end, salesforce.com has a double mission: Create a new business model on the commercial side and a new concept of corporate philanthropy on the foundation side, bolstered by strong team bonding.

Suzanne DiBianca, a former management consultant, signed on in early 2000 to head the salesforce.com Foundation, which coordinates salesforce.com's grants, in-kind donations, and employee efforts. "I saw the power that community service could have on a company as part of its long-term culture," she says. "I came in a little skeptical about Marc in the beginning, because there are a lot of people who talk about philanthropy as a way to talk about how much money they have. But Marc was serious about it. He had already set up a bank account just to run the foundation." DiBianca and her foundation team members sit in cubicles alongside the rest of the salesforce.com employees. Reports on community service projects are prominently featured in most company meetings.

Executives hired at salesforce.com can expect to be grilled not only on their business experience, but also on their philanthropic philosophy. DiBianca interviews top executive candidates before they join the company. If they're not committed to philanthropy, they get nixed. CFO Steve Cakebread, who was interviewed by Benioff and DiBianca before he was hired, recalls that he decided to join Salesforce for two reasons: "I liked the business model Marc was creating, and I liked the foundation. When you make [the idea of philanthropy] part of your interviewing and hiring, you get a group of people who are coming to work for more than just the paycheck," he adds. "It's a selling point when you're trying to recruit good people. It also sets the tone for what the company's about." As a member of the senior executive team, Cakebread quickly realized that Benioff and the company are serious in their commitment to philanthropy. "It's not just something written on a Web page," he says. "The fact that Marc personally funded the foundation [initially] and got these programs going so early is a testament to what we're trying to do."

Employee orientation at salesforce.com always includes a presentation on the foundation and its work; in fact, orientation will typically include an actual half day of service work at one of the 19 community centers at local schools and after-school programs that salesforce.com has equipped with computers and media labs. To date, 300 employees have given more than 5,000 hours of service. Once a salesforce.com office, say in Europe or Japan, reaches about 30–40 people, DiBianca will hire a dedicated foundation employee to begin coordinating local philanthropic activities. There is also an employee-based steering committee. Bryan Breckenridge, a sales account executive, says he already knew about the foundation from the company Website and specifically asked about it in his interview with former President John Dillon. "I knew this was the right company, partly because of that," he says. Breckenridge had told salesforce.com that, before he joined them, he wanted to spend a couple of months in India teaching English. "They sent me a commitment letter before I left," he says, proving that they were willing to wait for someone whose values matched the company's.

When Breckenridge or any of salesforce.com's executives make a presentation to a customer or a trade meeting, a few slides about the foundation's activities—particularly in funding and staffing the community centers at schools—almost inevitably pop up. Says Breckenridge, "About 10 percent of my slides in corporate presentations are about the foundation. It's a corollary benefit to being a company with this culture." In trying to sell the salesforce.com product, which is online customer relationship management software, "you have to be a person first and build relationships with the other person, who is your customer." Bringing up salesforce.com's work with schools "helps build rapport," says Breckenridge. "It gives you something human to talk about."

Culture of Giving

The experience at Oracle shows that no matter how generous the dollar figure is attached to corporate philanthropy, making it a part of the company culture won't just happen because someone writes a check. In fact, creating a culture of giving doesn't have as much to do with the cash donated as with the time and other resources donated. The company leadership must treat philanthropy with the same respect and attention that it gives to any other business activity, and set the example within the company for what can be done. It's especially eye-opening for employees when executives put in demonstrable effort, too, such as working on the front lines of a service project, serving on nonprofit boards, or leading fund-raising crusades. "If the executives are saying we cannot afford to do this, they're right," says Susan Colby, head of the Bridgespan Group's San Francisco office. (Bridgespan is the nonprofit arm of the consulting firm Bain & Co.) She adds that executives often ignite philanthropic efforts for personal reasons. "They're almost religious about the vision of what they think is possible. They can do extraordinary things if they want it badly enough."

Of course, keeping the business viable is the top priority for any corporation, but philanthropy can play a vital role in that effort by attracting the types of employees and customers and other stakeholders who value a whole company and a full life—employees such as Breckenridge and his direct-sales coworkers at salesforce.com, who give up many a Saturday to volunteer at company-sponsored events, or the ones at Timberland, who build homeless shelters during company events. At Hewlett-Packard Company, whose philanthropy will be profiled in

Chapters 9 and 10, Bill Hewlett and David Packard built more than a business. Packard always considered the "HP Way," which encompassed social responsibility before it was ever defined, to be his greatest innovation. A headline about him commented, "Packard executive develops company by design, calculator by accident." A well-designed company has a culture that embraces philanthropy, because it has an enlightened self-interest in improving the communities in which it resides. Community service also builds loyalty to the company, aligns ethical values with business values, allows employees to learn more skill, and fosters interdepartmental bonding. As DiBianca says, "You want to do philanthropy immediately to make it part of your culture. It's never too soon to start, but it can be too late to start."

Culturing Community Service

1. Leadership must come from the top, with verbal, financial, and resource commitments. If the leader participates in service activities, that's a great motivator.

2. Service should be a part of the corporation from the beginning, not left until the company gets big.

3. The head of the philanthropic effort, whether it's a foundation or corporate giving program, should regularly address company meetings to report on progress.

4. Employees should be allowed reasonable time off to perform community service, and this should be considered a positive, not a negative, in performance reviews.

5. Giving should be more than just dollars, including executive and employee time and expertise.

Defining a Mission

At most companies, corporate philanthropy typically gets started in one of two ways. The first way occurs when the CEO gets very passionate about a particular cause and decides to donate personal and/or corporate money to it. The second way is when the company decides that it needs to do philanthropy for PR/marketing reasons and begins making grants, either through a corporate giving program or a foundation. There are obvious flaws with both of these approaches. In the first, philanthropy never really becomes part of the culture, but is dependent upon the CEO's whim and can be turned off or on depending on his or her devotion to the cause. Even though passionate CEOs can do great things in charitable giving, there's a risk that the commitment may not survive the CEO's time at the top, especially in these days of rampant CEO turnover. Not only that, the CEO's passion may not fit well with the company's business, which again can cause philanthropy to sputter out if the CEO leaves or gets diverted by other issues.

In the second scenario, the company proclaims that it has, say, $500,000 or $1 million to give away, and is immediately inundated by requests from all sides. Every group, from schools to homeless shelters to outdoor theater companies to struggling artists, seeks a share of the largesse. The corporate philanthropy is largely reactive, responding to grant proposals, rather than proactive, putting in place a program that makes sense for the company and spelling out the types of projects it will consider. The motivation—to gain PR plaudits—is viewed as cynical by employees, so it does not engage them. Ultimately, the commitment is superficial and easily dislodged in difficult times.

One of the buzz terms in the philanthropy world these days is "strategic philanthropy," which refers to aligning charitable giving with a company's business mission, so that a technology company, for example, seeks to put computers in schools or provide Internet access within impoverished communities to bridge the digital divide. Strategic philanthropy, which will be discussed in more detail in Chapter 9, has its drawbacks too, but one thing it points up very well is the need for a clearly defined mission that drives philanthropic giving, just like the corporation's business side. This mission need not necessarily be strategic, but it should be something where the company can make an impact, not just with its checkbook, but with its employees and expertise. "The biggest mistake that corporations make [with philanthropy] is treating the subject too lightly," says Bob Goodwin, executive director of the Points of Light Foundation, established by George H.W. Bush to recognize the importance of community service by corporations and individuals. "We would advise companies that their philanthropic and workplace programs need to be interwoven into the fabric of the business," he adds. "If you treat it lightly, you don't provide the leadership, recognition, or the proper level of oversight and evaluation. You miss the opportunity to publicize the reason the program exists to begin with—to extend overall influence into the fabric of the community."

In the preceding chapter, we learned how a company such as Timberland can discover its mission somewhat serendipitously, and, indeed, for a company that's never done formalized philanthropy, experimenting with different approaches before settling on one or two can work out just fine. (For more on that, see Chapter 4.) However, many companies are finding that, in today's economy, it makes more sense to sit down with senior management (and, perhaps, with other stakeholders such as customers and community leaders) and work out a defined mission before undertaking a formal giving program. This is not to rule out such efforts as matching employee donations or joining the annual United Way drive; those are beneficial and should not be dismissed just because they don't adhere to a centralized mission. But for the corporation itself, and indeed for those who might seek grants from it, having a defined mission can save an awful lot of grief and misunderstanding. In this chapter, we outline the approaches that four very different companies took to defining their philanthropic missions.

BEA Systems, Inc.

San Jose-based BEA Systems, a 9-year-old company that makes software to help companies establish their Internet infrastructure, is low-key in its approach to philanthropy. So low-key that it sometimes doesn't get enough grant requests and has to approach community foundations to help find places to put its money. Nonetheless, the software company did do considerable introspection to determine what its philanthropic mission would be. And it's not what you'd expect—something such as Internet access, wiring schools, or providing its product to nonprofits. Rather, BEA concentrates on early childhood learning, believing that it is the foundation upon which everything else rests. Like many companies, BEA moved from an informal to formal philanthropic programming by starting a foundation in 2001 to codify what had been a rather directionless, yet strong conviction by the three founders to give something back. On that basis, they had done employee matches and allowed employees to take four hours a month off to do community service. BEA also had a donor-advised fund through Community Foundation Silicon Valley (CFSV), an intermediary agency that would take care of making grants with the company's money. (For more on intermediaries, see Chapter 12.)

But as it became a public company, grew past $1 billion in revenue, and expanded its scope across the globe, BEA wanted to take philanthropy under its own aegis. By having a foundation, "it's making a commitment to philanthropy rather than just saying that if we have extra money, we'll spend it in the community," says Diana Langeland, senior director of the BEA Foundation. "It's saying we're here for the long haul, so we won't be doing it hit or miss." The foundation was initially funded with $7 million in cash and BEA adds a percentage of profits every year. "When we started the foundation, I was convinced we would join the high-tech bandwagon and work on closing the digital divide," recalls Langeland. She formed an internal advisory council facilitated by Community Foundation Silicon Valley and had an intense meeting to define the mission of the new corporate foundation. The CFSV moderators advised Langeland that many companies do align their philanthropy with their mission. "What's your elevator pitch?" they asked. ("Elevator pitch" refers to the one-minute or so presentation that entrepreneurs give to venture capitalists and other potential investors and partners about a new company's purpose.) Langeland responded that BEA provides the foundation to help companies build their business. If you don't have a good foundation, it will hurt your business—BEA's selling point for its software. An employee on the advisory council who also happened to be a new mother raised her hand and remarked, "That's the same thing that you have to do with a child—build a strong foundation." That dovetailed very nicely with BEA's business message without overtly being about spreading technology, says Langeland, and, after approval from the executive team, "that became our funding focus. We have never deviated from that. You really don't want to have it spread all over the place."

BEA happened to start up its giving right after 9/11, and the first funded grantee was Rainbows, which was running a preschool program for children who had lost a close relative in the disaster. They also wanted to train teachers and counselors in how to deal with children who have suffered personal losses. "We gave them startup funding of $17,000 to create materials," says Langeland, and another $23,000 to roll out the program. One thing she's found with early learning is that you have to be patient. "I'm interested in things like getting more preschool teachers and more capacity for early learning," says Langeland. "My advisory council wants to fund direct services where they can see the immediate need." Having the mission statement about "developing and funding innovative programs that give our youngest children a strong start in life and a solid foundation for their future success" helps the council make its decisions. For instance, BEA recently joined the Newark (New Jersey) Lighthouse Initiative, which formed after New Jersey passed a law mandating that all preschools have to deliver the same quality of services, but didn't specify how. "We're providing funding for three model preschools that will provide the template for how other preschools can do it," says Langeland. The foundation also funds early literacy programs in San Jose, New York, Seattle, Boston, and Denver—all locations where the company has a presence.

To other companies wrestling with defining the scope of their philanthropy, Langeland cheers them on. "The most important thing you can do is, right from the start, be very specific in what you will and will not fund," she says. "It's the best thing for both [the corporate and nonprofit] sides."

LensCrafters, Inc.

LensCrafters, the largest optical retail chain, with 860 stores, kind of stumbled onto its mission—which is giving the gift of sight to needy people in North America and developing countries, by delivering free optical services and recycling used glasses. That mission is one that has worked brilliantly, both in involving employees and in drawing extraordinary attention for a company now buried within an Italian multinational, Luxottica Group. Most corporate philanthropy champions would tell you that it works better to decide on a focus for giving and then start laying out the bucks, and indeed that is a more efficient approach in the majority of cases. But LensCrafters's experience also shows that you can refine a mission on the fly, as it were, and ultimately come up with something unique and satisfying. Its program, Give the Gift of Sight, has twice received awards from the prestigious Points of Light Foundation: in 1994, for volunteer action, and in 1999, for excellence in corporate service.

Susan Knobler, now vice president of the LensCrafters Foundation, candidly admits that when she was in corporate communications in the mid-1980s, she was "fishing around for how to connect us to a cause. My earliest motivation was not pure. I was trying to get ink," she acknowledges. She decided to give away 25 pairs of glasses from a local store, which did earn some ink. So the program got expanded. "We started giving away more of our product. We'd have a busload of kids come into the store and we'd fit them all with glasses." That was expanded via a voucher program to other stores in the United States. Finally, LensCrafters teamed up with Lions Clubs International, which already had a program of collecting used glasses for people who couldn't afford to buy them. From those humble beginnings, Gift of Sight has morphed into an international program that, in 2002, delivered 39,000 pairs of new glasses to disadvantaged people who needed them; performed

20,000 eye exams for people in need; sent 286,000 employees and physicians into the community to deliver vision screenings, eyeglass adjustments, and repairs; sent Vision Vans to deliver optical services to 17,000 children in North America; performed 18,000 vision screenings in its hometown of Cincinnati; and hand-delivered and fitted newly cleaned, recycled glasses to 153,000 people in the Dominican Republic, Chile, Mexico, Guatemala, Bolivia, Laos, and Thailand.

Although Knobler was the internal champion for Gift of Sight, she acknowledges that the various CEOs of LensCrafters, as well as its new owner Luxottica, have all bought into the program in part because the "fit" is so perfect. In 1993, when LensCrafters was about to celebrate the 10th anniversary of its founding, the CEO challenged her to help 1 million people by the 20th anniversary. Because 11,000 people had been helped by the program the year before, "I thought he was being outrageously optimistic," she recalls. But by setting such a high goal, and putting the needed resources behind it, "he gave us permission to go do it." In fact, by its 20th birthday in 2003, LensCrafters had helped 3 million people since the formal founding of Gift of Sight in 1988. Knobler remembers a few of those 3 million individually, such as the small boy in Kenya who walked 10 miles to the LensCrafters clinic staring through a marble so he had enough light refraction to get there. In August 2001, a 64-year-old grandmother in Bolivia, Julia Gutierrez, became the 2 millionth "customer" of Gift of Sight. The first thing she did after receiving her glasses was rush home to see the faces of her twin granddaughters for the first time. LensCrafters employees are the ones who bring the glasses to clinics in overseas countries and fit them to the best recipients, with the help of physicians who also donate their time. (For more on how LensCrafters and other companies involve employees in philanthropy, see the next chapter.)

LensCrafters has also harnessed its business expertise to the Gift of Sight program by encouraging employees to figure out better ways to deliver glasses to those who need them. For example, the information technology department at LensCrafters figured out a way to computerize the tedious process of matching a used pair of glasses with the best person to receive them. Previously, a physician would write a prescription; then a picker would look through box after box of glasses to find the best match. "Someone in IT said if we could computerize this and let the computer pick, it would be better," says Knobler. Today, LensCrafters stores glasses collected from the Lions Clubs, and employees clean, repair, and classify them. The glasses are then shipped to the LensCrafters Foundation, which enters them into a database. On each mission to a foreign country, the employees take the donated glasses and half a dozen laptops loaded with a computer algorithm to match prescription to person. "The computer tells them, go to box 12 and take the 30th pair of glasses for this person," says Knobler. "It gives a first, second, and third choice in case some of the choices aren't available." People who can't be helped by glasses because they need surgery or some other kind of correction get a referral to Lions Clubs International, which works with LensCrafters to supply what is needed.

Knobler has a list of 10 principles that worked for LensCrafters and may assist others in designing a philanthropic program. Among those principles: "We focused our community service on our product....We harnessed our business expertise to fulfill our charitable objectives....We recognized and built on surprising new directions....We wove Gift of Sight into the fabric of the company....We persevered with passion and conviction." It all started with finding the right mission.

LensCrafters's 10 Principles for Making Philanthropy Successful

1. We focus our community service on our product, involving employees in hands-on giving experiences.

2. We keep our program non-promotional.

3. We brand our program with a strong, single identity—the Gift of Sight.

4. We push program ownership to the individual store level by empowering stores to choose their own charitable partners and invent their own local variations.

5. We have learned to forge partnerships, especially a long-term relationship with Lions Clubs International.

6. We set and track lofty program goals. Everyone knew the GOS goal was to help 3 million people by 2003. We have treated this as a corporate goal just like sales and profits.

7. We have developed and shared a GOS folklore to give the program emotional legs. We make a point of capturing magic moments and sharing them.

8. We harness our business expertise to fulfill charitable objectives.

9. We have recognized and built upon unexpected program benefits, such as extraordinary team-building and leadership experiences.

10. We weave this into the fabric of the company.

· · · · · · · · · · · · · · · · · · 🌍

Charles Schwab Corporation

Charles Schwab Corporation is one of those companies in which the founder's imprint was important in getting philanthropy going, but designing the mission came much later on. The San Francisco-based investment firm, founded in 1974, had the idea of letting the customer make his or her own investment choices, without requiring an account manager or advisor. The idea was to put the customer first. Carrie Schwab Pomerantz, president of the Charles Schwab Corporation Foundation (and daughter of Charles Schwab, who founded the company) says her father's beliefs certainly accounted for the company's business mission. "We were a company that was founded on the principle of democratizing investing," she says. "His idea was to challenge Wall Street and make things more accessible." At the same time, on the philanthropy front, Schwab, who was dyslexic as a child, was devoting personal wealth to the notion of helping families understand learning differences. "That was his personal passion," says Schwab, but it didn't make sense for the corporation to duplicate it.

For a while, then, Schwab's corporate philanthropy was in a state of drift. The company knew it wanted to do philanthropy, but it wasn't clear how. The Foundation was started 10 years ago, "primarily as a way to provide an employee matching gift program," Pomerantz says. "Meanwhile, over the years we had never really had a strategy for our funding, except for areas where our employees would rally around something." This led to a lot of discretionary—that is, reactive—giving, but the overall program lacked focus, she acknowledges, not that the employee matching was without its rewards, because discretionary matching allows employees to follow their passion. Says Pomerantz, "Employees are our most important resource. Employee service is a great morale booster, building teamwork and leadership skills. Then we make a bigger impact by matching their gifts." But when Pomerantz took over the Foundation in 2002, in the midst of a brutal economic downturn both in Schwab's geographic home in the San Francisco Bay Area and in its field of financial services, she decided it was a time for reflection and planning. Out of that came a refocused mission for philanthropy that is just starting to make an impact.

"I took the Foundation through strategic planning to give ourselves a mission," says Pomerantz. Out of that came two areas of focus: continuing to support employee causes, which had been very popular with the employees, and a corporate strategy of helping at-risk teens, young adults, and other disadvantaged groups achieve financial literacy. "That's where we're going to be focusing all our resources from now on," says Pomerantz. "You can give more value with what you've got if you're focused. We're trying to bring our time, our expertise, our technology, our advocacy to an area where we can create generational changes." Early on, she adds, the group came up with another mission that was a very nice play on words: "helping every individual become a community investor." It sounded great, but when Pomerantz and her team tried to use it to designate grants, "people didn't understand what it mean. It was a lofty mission, because it would imply we're going to help the world, but it was not clear or concise. Employees didn't know what we were committing to."

However, helping the disadvantaged achieve financial literacy fit in well with Schwab's initial reason for being, as well as with goals that both father and daughter wanted to achieve. Under that aegis, which just was put in place about a year ago, Schwab has donated to Jumpstart, a financial literacy program for kids, and helped them create a Website in

California. It has donated office space and computers to various organizations that do work in financial literacy. It has donated a library of
books on investing to a program at the San Quentin prison. Pomerantz,
who defines her own personal passion as economic parity for women,
finds that that can fit into the new corporate philanthropy mission as
well. She serves on the board of a newly created San Francisco international museum for women, which includes the financial aspects of their
lives. Schwab gave $25,000 to get the exhibit up and running, and now
the group is in the process of putting together a permanent museum.
Pomerantz testified before the governing Board of Supervisors to tell
them how committed Schwab was to the notion of a museum dedicated
to women's history worldwide; she believes that kind of networking
helped the museum get governmental and corporate support. At
Schwab, corporate giving amounts to $5 million a year, roughly 1 percent
of net profits, with an additional $1.6 million in employee matching.
"We've always been one of those cultures where we live by and breathe
our values," says Pomerantz. Focused corporate giving, she believes,
reinforces that.

eBay, Inc.

Like Cisco, eBay was another of those fabulous Silicon Valley success stories. Founded in 1995, eBay developed a unique, Internet-based
model for auctioning off goods of all kinds, becoming the electronic
equivalent of the garage sale. Initially, eBay did its giving through a
donor-advised fund at Community Foundation Silicon Valley (similar
to what BEA did), but as the company grew larger and became a blazing
Internet star, it decided to take the giving in-house. In the 1998 initial
public offering, eBay had already endowed a corporate foundation with
about $1 million worth of stock—107,250 shares; today that stock is
worth $30 million. In June 2002, the company tapped Irene Wong, who
had been director of corporate services at Community Foundation Silicon
Valley, to run the foundation and carve out its mission. Before Wong
came on board, the giving at eBay was "very typical," she recalls, "driven
by whatever nonprofits wrote in for grants and sounded interesting." Each
quarter there would be a different theme, like youth initiatives or
healthcare. One project helped women in a Guatemalan village sell their
handicrafts, such as woven belts, on eBay.

But one of Wong's imperatives was to define a mission for the foundation. To do so, "we took the over-arching values of eBay, such as building online communities, developing alternative markets of buyers and sellers, and using the auction as a means of self-sufficiency and cutting out the middleman, and wove in what we thought were important community issues," she says. Among the guiding principles: "We invest in high-leverage programs that provide individuals with tools, skills, training, motivation, and support that will improve their lives and their communities," and "we invest in organizations that have lasting, positive impact and maximize the ability to transform the world." Out of those principles came four areas in which eBay Foundation would make grants: community technology, community economic development, community strengthening, and community participation. Because eBay's community of 62 million users is worldwide, grants can be awarded in virtually any location, although there is some emphasis on locations where the company has offices. For example, eBay's Foundation Technology Prize emphasizes developing nations, rural poor, seniors, children, and other underserved groups. With community economic development, eBay supports microloans that "enable people to raise their standard of living and fully participate in the global economy." Similarly, community strengthening aims to assist artisans, such as the women in Guatemala, in getting their wares to a broad market, providing an income stream for people and their community. Finally, community participation encourages volunteerism, particularly from eBay employees, by doing matching gifts and recognizing organizations that are championed by employees.

Starting in 2003, the foundation was planning to make $1.5–$1.7 million worth of grants annually to its four focus areas. "We were reactive," says Wong. "Now we want to take a long view and put strategy behind our giving." One example was SeniorNet, a San Francisco-based non-profit that works with existing senior centers to help older people get online; eBay gave a $1-million grant to create 10 computer labs to bring technology to seniors. "At the same time we provided the seniors with information on how to sell on eBay," says Wong. Because many older people downsize at retirement, moving from a larger to a smaller home, being able to sell their excess goods on eBay is both a financial and a practical benefit. One man in Salt Lake City has developed a whole new supplemental income by selling goods of his own and other people on eBay. Ann Wrixon, the president of SeniorNet, says eBay's grant was particularly welcomed because many corporate givers want to invest in youth or education, so older adults get lost. Having a well-known company such as eBay on board "tends to attract other funders," she says. "It's so unusual for a young technology company to be funding seniors."

In an effort to tap into the expertise and desires of its customers, eBay has set up a committee of users to suggest where else it might give, says Wong, although that effort is just getting off the ground. "We're real excited, because our biggest asset is our 62 million users," she says. "We're trying to figure out how to leverage that for greater community benefit."

Mission Possible

Although many corporate foundations and giving programs continue to do much good through what eBay's Wong calls "reactive" programs, the operative word today in corporate philanthropy is focus. Defining a mission first of all helps the corporation figure out where it will give and why and enables the giving to have greater and more lasting impact. It also helps the nonprofits who might seek grants from the company to determine where they fit and how to structure their proposals. Of course, the flip side of focus means that some deserving organizations may find themselves out in the cold as companies refine their philanthropic missions. In particular, arts groups seem to be affected by corporate decisions to narrow their concentration to areas where they can have the most impact. The increased corporate emphasis on focus may compel nonprofits to do the same, to rethink their missions in a way that fits new priorities. For example, rather than simply subsidize the purchase of paintings for a museum or provide funding for opera or symphony, an arts group could develop programs that encourage more diversity in attendance by sponsoring special events attractive to children or to minorities. In fact, Susan Colby of the nonprofit consulting firm Bridgespan Group believes that corporate focus may, in the long run, aid nonprofits, because they can get larger grants from fewer funders. "Nonprofits spend a huge amount of time raising money in inefficient ways," she says, such as increments of

$500 or $1,000. By finding corporate partners who are "serious about their mission," nonprofits may be able to improve their own fund-raising efficiency.

Even with a very well-defined mission, corporations are never going to become entirely proactive in their giving. They'll still listen to their employees and provide funding to causes that inspire workers and customers and other stakeholders. They'll still respond to emergencies in the communities they serve, such as a natural disaster or an economic reversal. Companies with focused philanthropy tend to keep a certain percentage of unallocated funds on hand for such events, 9/11 being one of the primary examples. Salesforce.com, for example, devotes 80 percent of its funding to its designated mission—technology and youth—and reserves 20 percent to match employee giving and to respond to emergencies. After all, we live in an unpredictable world, and companies don't want to become so rigid that they can't respond to the crying needs of that world.

Involving Employees

Corporations routinely boast that their employees are their most valuable assets. In research-intensive industries such as technology and biotech, in fact, hostile takeovers are rare, in part, because the crown jewels of the company can walk out of the door in their tennis shoes. So when it comes to philanthropy, why not leverage that same asset? First of all, it allows the corporation to leverage a grant or in-kind gift by supplying specialized expertise to go along with it. Many businesses, for example, donate computers to schools or nonprofits, but without skilled employee IT labor to help set up those computers, they often wind up shoved into a corner or a closet. Employees can harness their business and management skills by serving on nonprofit boards or heading up important public/private partnership efforts such as IBM's "Reinventing Education" or Hewlett-Packard Company's "Digital Village." (For more on large, multiyear projects, see Chapter 11.) Having Corporate America working alongside the nonprofit sector facilitates an exchange of ideas and knowledge that can benefit both sides.

Beyond the benefits to the nonprofit sector, the corporation also gains when its employees are engaged in philanthropic endeavors. "There are a range of business benefits for employee involvement, including leadership development, such as taking shop-floor personnel and giving them coordination or management responsibility that sharpens and develops new skills," says Bob Goodwin, executive director of the Points of Light Foundation. Employees involved in these activities gain increased esteem and better morale. Furthermore, "having people from up and down the organization working side by side in a community project will serve to lessen tensions that might develop between union and management," Goodwin adds, "diminishing barriers that could confound workplace dynamics and making it easier to relate to one another as peers." Then, of course, there are all the marketing advantages of putting people on the line in community activities. "When the community sees the company as not simply taking profits out of the community, but putting people and resources into the community, that strengthens the company's reputation as a good corporate citizen," he says. The community may express its appreciation through awards or write-ups in publication or letters that contribute to that all-important feeling of self-esteem that's a cherished part of being human. "Sometimes the appreciation (for nonprofit work) is among the most plentiful the employee receives," Goodwin says. "It helps employees feel better about themselves and the company."

Previously, we described how establishing a culture of philanthropy, which flows down from the top, and defining a mission can make it easier for a corporation to do projects and set an example that inspires employees to get involved in them. In this chapter, we show some hands-on techniques for fully engaging employees in philanthropic projects, ranging from rewarding them with trips to deliver donated products overseas to providing funding to match "sweat equity" to generally keeping service as a centerpiece of the company's overall mission. A couple of the companies described here, salesforce.com and LensCrafters, appeared in earlier chapters, but because culture, mission, and involving employees are so closely intertwined, it makes sense to see the entire pattern of how these "best practices" companies go about it.

Cadence Design Systems, Inc.

Formed in 1988 through the merger of two other companies, Cadence provides electronic design technologies and services to the microprocessor and hardware industries. In other words, its products are used to design the chips that may reside inside your car or your digital cable box or your computer. It's a kind of behind-the-scenes company that doesn't get a lot of public acclaim for its product line, nor does the latter lend itself to the high-profile in-kind giving that many technology companies can do. "Cadence doesn't have a wonderful product we can donate to nonprofits," says Kathy Wheeler, Cadence's global community affairs manager, because most nonprofits don't need arcane equipment to design chips. Instead, Cadence focuses on leveraging its name, primarily through its annual bowling gala, called Stars & Strikes, and its 5,000 employees. Stars & Strikes, which raised $1.2 million in 2002, takes grant proposals from the community in selected areas—for helping women and children and for education—and then uses an employee grants committee to narrow down the proposals. An executive team decides among the finalists.

In communities where Cadence has a presence, employees are able to take a portion of the Stars & Strikes funds raised locally and apply it to a project of their choice. For example, in 2001 the Cadence facility outside New Delhi raised funds from a cricket tournament under the auspices of "Spirit of Stars & Strikes" (bowling not being particularly popular in India). Cadence CEO Ray Bingham and his wife recently went to visit India and see for themselves the orphanage for local children built by combining the funds raised from the cricket event with employee labor. In the middle of a very impoverished area, a "tent city," as Bingham put it, "this orphanage is a two-story whitewashed building with some grass and trees inside a little enclosure." Compared with what's around it, it looks like a veritable palace, very clean and utilitarian. When the Binghams visited, the children, ages 2 to 15, all wore their Sunday best. "This is a perfect model of how we want our philanthropy to work," says Bingham, with local employees seeing a need and filling it, helped by some matching funding from the corporation.

The team didn't just build the orphanage and then disengage, says Saugat Sen, a Cadence employee in India. "The one fundamental theme was to make a difference to underprivileged children," he says. "This provides a meaningful avenue for people to fulfill their social responsibility, but it also provides a new sense of belonging to the organization." Employees continue to work with the orphanage children, teaching them about computers, reading to them, helping them with their English.

51

"I've gotten personally involved as a sponsor in making this happen," he says. Not only that, the orphanage, which was designed by the same architect who did the Cadence building, continues to stand as a symbol of Cadence's community involvement and inspires the children to dream. Last year, the India team did another cricket tournament and raised enough funds to provide education and healthcare for 2,000 children for a year. "We stay engaged in how the money's used and there's a lot of excitement generated among the employees in learning the stories of those who benefit," says Sen.

Closer to home, in Cadence's San Jose headquarters and other U.S. sites, employees organize various fund-raising activities that revolve around Stars & Strikes. In 2002–3 "we wanted to make a difference in the life of a child," recalls employee Teri Gouveia, who works in Chelmsford, Massachusetts. "All our activities were centered around benefiting children." They raised money and provided labor to spruce up the Paul Center, a year-round camp for children with special needs. One of the fund-raising activities was having a dunk tank where all the executives participated. "The employees loved that," recalls Gouveia. You could sense her smiling even via a telephone conference call. Another favorite activity was doing a half-day service project at the camp, building additional cabins, repairing the dock, and meeting the children. "We found that very rewarding," she says. "You can just write a check or give your time, get involved at any level." But she thinks personal involvement is the best, because you get to "meet the recipients face-to-face and become a champion for them."

The executives generally participate in the employee-designed fundraisers. Besides getting dunked in a tank, they've had pies thrown in their faces and dressed up as spooks and goblins for Halloween booths. "It's not an ivory tower around here," says employee Dina Spencer. "Executives are just people like us who are doing their best." She adds that philanthropy has been instilled as part of Cadence's culture. "I've been here since there were 100 of us. There's always been this belief that people at Cadence can make a difference." She recalled an employee who had been laid off and was being escorted out on her last day, who stopped to make her contribution to Stars & Strikes. "People still want to make a difference."

LensCrafters, Inc.

As described in the previous chapter, the centerpiece of LensCrafters's philanthropy is its Gift of Sight (GOS) program, which has provided glasses, eye exams, and other services to 3 million people since its beginning in 1988. As it has grown exponentially, GOS has involved the majority of LensCrafters's 18,000 employees, according to Susan Knobler, vice president of the company foundation that oversees the program. Employees man the vision vans that go around to neighborhoods providing optical exams and free glasses, they devise special community outreach events at local stores, and they travel overseas to examine and fit impoverished people with recycled glasses collected in a partnership with the Lions Clubs International. The overseas trips especially provide great leadership and diversity training, Knobler believes, because employees are working in unfamiliar environments with ad hoc teams of associates, whom they probably don't know, and helping recipients from different cultures and backgrounds. "What better way to teach teamwork, flexibility, creativity, and the power of a positive attitude than to take 25 like-minded adults to a developing country for two weeks and challenge them to deliver eye exams and recycled glasses to 25,000 local people—knowing they will face electric outages, equipment held up in customs, unfamiliar food, and strange accommodations," she says. "On 54 missions to 25 developing countries, our teams have figured out how to work together to overcome obstacles. This learning is transferable to their stores and their lives."

Recent missions have gone to Tunisia, Chile, Costa Rica, Thailand, the Dominican Republic, Laos, Mexico, Guatemala, Peru, and Bolivia. In applying to participate in a GOS Mission Team, as the overseas groups are called, employees fill out a form that indicates what other philanthropic activities they've participated in, what languages they speak, and other community activities they've done. The supervisor also rates the employee's performance and strengths and weaknesses. Knobler says employees must earn the right to join in the highly sought-after overseas missions, which allow them to spend about two weeks in a foreign country. First, employees might staff the vision van or participate in the "hometown day" events on the first Wednesday of each December, when LensCrafters's 860 stores give away glasses and do other community events, such as auctions and raffles, to raise money for GOS. "What the overseas trips do is help us develop a career progression in volunteerism; there's a goal to shoot for," she says. "You work your way up to an overseas mission, which is financed by the foundation and company." The foundation raises about $1 million in cash annually, a quarter of which is donated by employees, and $2 million in goods for the GOS efforts.

Beyond the numbers are the memories that employees bring back with them. In a mission to the Philippines in 1996, Ray Grimball, a general manager in Alpharetta, Georgia, recalls helping a woman with such poor vision that no glasses matched her prescription. "One innovative team member super-glued our two highest minus lenses together and filed them by hand to fit her frame," he says. Then the team tried to determine if she could see by having her read a nearby sign. But she had been so nearsighted her entire life that she had never learned to read. Instead, "she looked up at our Gift of Sight sign and started to trace it with her fingers," he says. "We instantly realized she could see! There wasn't a dry eye in the entire clinic." Tom Phillpot, director of advertising/media for LensCrafters, went on a mission to Guatemala in 2002 and fitted a 3-year-old boy with glasses. The boy was expressionless until Phillpot put the glasses on him. "Suddenly, the biggest smile lit up his face. He looked at me, his mother, at everyone in the clinic. He instantly got the giggles; his new glasses seemed to change his world," he says. Dr. Mark Crafford, a LensCrafters optometrist in Virginia Beach, Virginia, went on a 1997 mission to Peru and remembers people sleeping in line for days, for the opportunity to see an eye doctor. "Our visit is often a once-in-a-lifetime chance to get glasses, so they will do whatever it takes to get to our clinic," he says. "We put a pair of glasses on one little Peruvian girl and tears started rolling down her face. That alone is enough to make you keep coming back."

For two years, LensCrafters has been named to *Fortune* magazine's top 100 U.S. companies to work for, in part, because, according to the magazine, employees "raved about working for a company with philanthropic impulses." Notes Chief Operating Officer Cliff Bartow, "What began as an altruistic effort turned out to help us internally on so many levels. It has been key in building strong teams, training committed leaders, and recruiting good people. It's tough to say who benefits most—those who receive donated eyecare or those who deliver it." Scott Brown, a LensCrafters IT specialist and a veteran of several overseas missions, says going on one makes you want to do more. "The sense of common purpose is so strong that you return with an indelible understanding of what collaboration and teamwork in practice mean," he says. "This translates directly into the workplace and leads to much more productive work relationships all around." Brown, who has been offered positions at other companies, says he has stayed at LensCrafters, in part, because GOS has meant so much to him both professionally and personally. "I'm just not willing to give it up."

Salesforce.com

On an unusually bright Saturday morning in May 2003, 15 members of the salesforce.com sales team showed up in San Francisco's Chinatown district, squinting in the sunlight. They weren't there as tourists (although with the struggling local economy, Chinatown could probably use that), but as balloon blowers, game referees, food-sellers, and other types of booth volunteers at the first annual Honey Bee Jamboree. It's a community carnival staged at the Jean Parker Elementary School—also home to one of the 19 technology centers for youth that salesforce.com has equipped in its headquarters city. Bryan Breckenridge, one of salesforce.com's most ardent champions of philanthropy, and his wife Linzi are among the volunteers. So is Jamie Grenney, a salesperson who joined the company about a year ago. "It's tough to get a real grasp on what philanthropy means until you come out to something like this and see for yourself," he remarks. Breckenridge is bouncing to the music of a samba band as he hands out hot dogs and chips at the food booth. "This is a chance for kids who never have grass to play on to come out and have some fun," he says. Inside the school's recreation hall, there is bingo for adults; white elephant sales; games such as ring toss, golf putt, and basketball; and demonstrations of origami (shaping paper) and face painting. Janet Dong, the school principal, passes through the crowd, urging people to take a piece of candy from her basket. Although the school was built in 1911, Principal Dong comments that "this is the first time we've ever done something like this." She says a large part of that is due to salesforce.com and its employees: "Because of salesforce.com, we have a computer lab. Because of salesforce.com, we have the manpower to do this today....It has always been my dream to do things like this, but you cannot do it by yourself."

The event in Chinatown represents a slight evolution in salesforce.com's approach to involving employees. From the beginning of salesforce.com, we decided to allow employees to dedicate 1 percent of their time—about four hours a month or six days a year—to do philanthropic work. Roughly half the employees take advantage of that, according to Suzanne DiBianca, executive director of the salesforce.com Foundation. On the company's dime (at least for the first four hours a month), employees can volunteer at charitable organizations or sign up to participate in numerous events coordinated by the foundation, such as the one in Chinatown. DiBianca says she's always had great support for philanthropy from the top executives at salesforce.com and from rank-and-file employees, but not so much from middle managers, who, of course, are concerned about meeting project deadlines and the impact of losing employee time to service projects. "The weakest part of our philanthropy today is middle management," DiBianca acknowledges, especially in terms of participation. "Getting them out [on a project] is hard," she says, "so I'm testing a new model." In that model, different departments at salesforce.com "adopt" one of the technology centers and become its designated source of volunteers. The sales team took the Jean Parker Elementary School center, which is why they gave up a Saturday morning for the kids' carnival. They'll also visit the center itself periodically, provide technical support if needed, mentor the kids on their various media or computer projects, and just get to know the operation. "We're embedded at the grassroots level," says DiBianca of salesforce.com's philanthropic effort. "Now I have to move it up to engage middle management." By directly pairing a department with a technology center and devising less time-consuming projects, she hopes to accomplish that.

Much of the employees' involvement revolves around the technology centers—19 in San Francisco and 22 elsewhere in the United States and overseas, including Israel, Ireland, India, Nepal, Kenya, and Romania. The typical model for the centers is for the salesforce.com Foundation to donate equipment and fund the start-up, plus dedicate two staff members to provide ongoing technical support and training, mentoring, program consulting, and other services. Salesforce.com's own server hosts youthspace.net, a Website that provides a showcase for youth media projects created at the technology centers, including video, music, photography, short stories, and reviews. The Beacon Center at AP

Giannini Middle School in San Francisco is typical. Inside a large room are about 30 computes, where several kids are working, plus other types of equipment such as digital cameras and recorders. "Salesforce.com was the local partner to start the program," says Michael Funk, founder and director of the center. "They brought in people to work with us and figure out program development. They realized that the biggest issue with technology isn't the hardware but how to integrate it with what we do." At the center, the kids use the equipment in connection with extra-curricular activities such as the DJ Club, which produces radio shows; the Small Business Club, which does electronic financial statements; and the Music Club, which creates online compositions. Bamboozled.org, a Website written and designed by youth at the center, is hosted by salesforce.com. "We're the only community center that got nominated for a Webby award," says Funk proudly, in recognition of bamboozled.org.

Salesforce.com also regularly brings groups of youth into its office to give them technology and career training. In April 2003, the company brought in 14 students, mostly African-American and Latino, from McLymonds High School in Oakland, to teach them how to design a Website. The kids were participants in the "I Have a Dream" project that prepares them for their futures. Several salesforce.com employees were on hand to help with the project, which consisted of brainstorming about a Website aimed at teenagers dealing with issues related to HIV/AIDS. Two women from marketing talked to one group of students about the content of a Website and how to appeal to the intended audience, while two salesforce.com programmers tutored other interested students in HTML coding. "We have to figure out relevant ways for our employees to work with kids," says Steve Wright, program director for the salesforce.com Foundation. Besides teaching skills such as building a Website, "what it's really about is possibilities," broadening the students' horizons by showing them what the options are for them in the technology industry. "Employee support from companies is very important to the program," adds Lois McKinney, community service coordinator for the "I Have a Dream" project. "The kids get the opportunity to see that somebody in the workforce cares enough about them to volunteer their time and share what they know and how they got where they are."

Soup's on at Raphael House

"I consider myself a huge a**hole most of the time," says Frank Defesche candidly, as we travel to a salesforce.com service project arranged at the Raphael House shelter in San Francisco. Preparing a meal for a dozen homeless families makes him feel like a little bit less of an a**hole. "I spend too much of my life doing stuff for me. Here I'm doing something for my own conscience. I feel better about myself."

Defesche and the other half dozen people who went to Raphael House in early June 2002 on a cool day that passes for spring in San Francisco look like poster children for the technology revolution. They are young, trim, energetic, ethnically diverse, and casually prosperous. Despite the dot-com bust a couple of years previously, start-up technology companies are still sucking in smart young people such as these with the same dream: build a company, change the world, and, incidentally, get rich in the process.

But at salesforce.com, there is another dream: enthroning community service as a centerpiece of building a great company. Salesforce.com employees, like the seven who trouped to Raphael House, can take paid time off to do volunteer work, either of their own choosing or arranged by the company. Raphael House, suggested by one of salesforce.com's engineers, has become a favorite. Geographically, it's not far from salesforce.com's headquarters in the downtown Embarcadero District, across the street from the famed Ferry Building. Psychologically, Raphael House, located in a converted hospital in the hardscrabble, impoverished Tenderloin area, seems like a different country.

The seven people there to prepare a meal for the less fortunate were all, except for one, out of their element in Raphael House's large, homey kitchen. Along with Defesche, the group included Sven Mawson, Ryan Choi, Chris Hopkins, Marcus Jessup, John Jordano, and Bala Subramanian, the only woman. They were all in their late

20s to mid-30s; devoted to their jobs as programmers, sales-people, or consultants for salesforce.com; and interested in doing something that will take them outside those jobs for an afternoon.

The task was to fix meat loaf, potatoes, Caesar salad, vegetable medley, dinner rolls, and chocolate cake in enough quantity for the 50 people expected at the evening's meal. Except for Subramanian, who worked in her college cafeteria, none of the rest of them had a clue as to how to proceed. Fortunately for them, and for the 50 people, they were supervised by Raphael House's regular cook, Isaac, an affable African-American, who was accustomed to shepherding well-meaning volunteers.

Isaac quickly split them up into small teams—no difference here, really, from a technology company—to tackle each portion of the meal. As they worked, they talked. Subramanian, an engineering manager, could take time away from the office that day because salesforce.com had no immediate deadline for a new release. "You always think about doing this kind of thing and you always say, 'when it's convenient,'" she said. Salesforce.com made it convenient. "Giving money is too easy. Donating to Goodwill is too easy," she said, and besides, you never come in contact with the people you're helping. At Raphael House, they would also serve the food when it's ready, and make a human connection, not just a tax-deductible donation.

"This is the first time I ever volunteered for anything," Hopkins said. "I thought I could use some karma. I tend to be a very selfish person."

In the specter of a bad economy, with thousands of coworkers and peers out of work, no one is as sure of the right of prosperity. Laboring at Raphael House brings a needed sense of giving back. The unspoken hope is that our own luck, or "karma" as Hopkins calls it, will be enhanced by the good deed.

Along with building the company, salesforce.com's intent is to build an army of compassion. In 10 years, if optimistic forecasts are correct, the company could be doing $10 billion in sales and have 10,000 employees, many giving time to service projects. At that point, Defesche will be taking a new generation to Raphael House and showing them how he changed his life.

—Karen Southwick

. . . . ⊕

Motivating Employees

Involving employees in philanthropic endeavors is a pure win-win for a corporation. To be sure, there could be slight trade-offs in the hours that employees spend on the job, but four hours a month or so spent in community service—a typical benchmark—is hardly going to impact performance. It may even improve it by giving employees some much needed "time out" to rediscover other aspects of life beyond the job. Even in an economic downturn, people are still motivated to do good, perhaps even more so than during boom years such as the late 1990s. Offering an opportunity for service may not be sufficient to retain a good employee, but it certainly helps. And, hopefully, such opportunities not only help employees gain new skills in leadership, teamwork, and thinking out of the box, but create a more well-rounded human being.

At salesforce.com, we believe that service is an essential and critical part of our architecture, drawing employees who want to be a part of that. People are more fulfilled and better off for doing this work. Their lives are more integrated. Not only is salesforce.com giving them a job, but also a path to service in their community. Years ago, when people lived in small groups or towns, such as an Amish community, they knew that service was a part of their life. Most of us don't have that kind of life anymore, but we instinctively know that we need it. That's why programs such as LensCrafters's Gift of Sight and Cadence's Stars & Strikes mean so much, not just to the people they help, but perhaps even more to those doing the helping.

Starting Small

oday, most companies that start philanthropic endeavors want to make an immediate impact, and they often think they can do that only if they have big bucks to give in grants. But, in fact, corporate philanthropy's important contributions are not dollars alone—corporate giving represents about 5 percent of the overall total in the United States, including individuals and private foundations. As we've shown in the previous three chapters, enlisting employees in corporate giving efforts and providing expertise and product donations not available elsewhere can be as valuable to nonprofits as money itself. So small companies or startups certainly do not need to feel inadequate about engaging in philanthropy. As indicated in Chapter 1, encouraging service as soon as possible after a company's founding builds it into the culture in a way that can't be extracted from the DNA, even as circumstances change down the road. Trying to add it later, even though the company may have far greater resources, never works as well. Grafted-in cultural elements never fully take root.

"If you want to be an outstanding corporate citizen, it makes sense to have a vision from the get-go," says David Vidal, director of research on global corporate citizenship for The Conference Board. "If you do it as an add-on, it will show. It's like raising a child and trying to inculcate something at 15." Dori Ives, a longtime philanthropy and marketing consultant in Silicon Valley, adds that she advises companies to do philanthropy from "they day they get started, in terms of developing it as a corporate value and business priority." That doesn't require setting up a $100-million foundation immediately. Instead, it can mean something as simple as a matching gift program of $1,000 per employee or paid time off. "The important thing is to start with a program that reflects your business interests, responds to community needs, and involves employees," Ives says. "If you have people power and add a few bucks to that, the company looks good and it's a win-win for you and the community." Dinah Waldsmith, senior manager for Business for Social Responsibility, a San Francisco-based, nonprofit consulting firm, agrees with Ives. "Even if it's just a food or toy drive around Christmas, do something that people in the company can feel good about," she says. "Employees expect the company they work for, no matter how small, to be involved with the community outside."

The three examples that are profiled here are all still small, non-public companies: Application Technologies Incorporated, known as AppsTech, based in Washington, D.C.; Craigslist, an electronic classified advertising service based in San Francisco; and Propel Software Corporation, a San Jose company founded by serial entrepreneur and philanthropist Steve Kirsch. What they have in common are entrepreneurs who had a vision of philanthropy from day one and found a way to combine that vision with building a company.

10 Ways for Small (and Large) Companies to Give

At salesforce.com, we give to our community in the following ways:

1. Donating money, in the form of grants and employee matching.

2. Giving time, from employees and executives.

3. Offering nonprofits the use of products and consulting related to that.

4. Facilitating the donation of goods from employees—everything from baseball cards to clothes to baby formula.

5. Providing nonprofits with professional assistance, such as financial and public relations expertise.

6. Offering technical training in areas such as networking, computer lab management, and the like.

7. Providing curriculum for school and after-school programs.

8. Hosting Websites and domain names for nonprofits.

9. Providing use of computers, office equipment, and meeting space.

10. Encouraging executives and employees to sit on nonprofit boards.

· · · · · · · · · · · · · · · · · · · 🌐

AppsTech

AppsTech CEO Rebecca Enonchong is an extraordinary rarity in the technology industry—indeed, in any industry. A native of Cameroon, Africa, she came to the United States to get her B.S. and master's degree in Economics from the Catholic University of America, and started out in consulting. She has done financial work for Hyatt Hotels, the Washington Business Group, and the Inter-American Development Bank. In 1999, she decided to found her own company, AppsTech, which helps corporations set up complex business applications. While building her company to around 100 employees, Enonchong remains devoted to promoting African interests, both inside and outside AppsTech. She is founder of the Africa Technology Forum (run by full-time employees of her company) and serves on an advisory committee for the U.N. Development Fund for Women. A recipient of Enterprise Africa's 2001 African Entrepreneurship Award, Enonchong was also named a Global Leader for Tomorrow by the World Economic Forum of Davos, Switzerland, which recognizes outstanding leaders around the world.

About a year after she started AppsTech, Enonchong attended an event for entrepreneurs from India, who are legion in the technology industry, and wondered, *why can't we do the same thing for Africa?* To that end, she started the Africa Technology Forum as a 501(c)(3) non-profit organization and paid two employees to work there full-time. Those employees are on the payroll of the Forum, but AppsTech pays the salaries. Other employees participate in the Forum on an as-needed basis. The mission of the Forum is to promote technology entrepreneurship in Africa, she says. "We're not trying to bridge the digital divide. We look beyond that. We believe Africa can be a center for technology innovation—developing applications and hardware." The Forum, with an annual budget of $500,000—primarily funded by AppsTech, with some contributions—has three strategic initiatives. The first is to convince the African public of the value of technology by staging informational events that people can attend. The second goal is to increase the number of technology professionals in Africa by 300,000 in three years. It's unclear how big an increase that will be, but it's presumably substantial. "We're developing a database of all the existing technology professionals in Africa now," Enonchong says. Much of this effort will be concentrated around education. For example, AppsTech partnered with one of its business partners, Oracle Corporation, to offer training in database administration in Cameroon. "There were no computers, no books, just explanatory material from the teacher," she says. "There were about 600 people who took the class." Enonchong explains that the lack of infrastructure in Africa should not deter learning. "Oral tradition is strong in Africa," she says. "It's important to understand how we learn, how we think and interact with each other." Finally, the third goal is to create a better technology-enabling environment for would-be entrepreneurs by working with governments and regulatory agencies. One project is an incubator for entrepreneurs to create cutting-edge technology as a showcase for what Africans can do. Another effort is a mentor program in collaboration with the World Economic Forum to encourage technology entrepreneurs in Africa, especially women. The mentors are successful U.S. and European entrepreneurs who donate their time. Starting in late 2003, the Forum plans to publish the Africa Technology Index, which ranks African companies based on their technology-enabling environments.

Enonchong, who estimates that she spends about a fifth of her time on the Forum, encourages employees to participate as well. For example, AppsTech IT employees maintain and host the Forum Website. Marketing and public relations staff get involved in promoting the activities. Engineers and software consultants act as mentors to their counterparts in Africa. All of them learn about the Forum before joining the company. On the day she spoke with me, Enonchong had made a presentation to an employee orientation session about the Forum. Although AppsTech doesn't have a formal policy of paid time off, if employees want to go work with one of the activities in Africa, they make arrangements to cover their daily work and "just go," Enonchong says. Many of the ideas for what to do with the forum come from employees, such as the entrepreneur incubator. "When I was talking with the employees, they came up instantly with tons of ideas and contacts who could help the incubator," she says. "We have a team of employees working to get the incubator together."

At the same time, the CEO/founder recognizes her duty to her company. "We're profitable now and we want to stay that way," she says. But there are many payoffs from employees' work with the forum, Enonchong maintains. "I've loved to see how people have grown and developed and become leaders," as they tackle projects outside their usual venue. In addition, she's already employing skilled workers in Africa and expects to hire more of them. "I'm hoping that out of Africa we'll see leaders and entrepreneurs," she says. "Regardless of what field they get involved in, they can take that training [that they get from us] and use it to lead the way, whether in the public or private sector." The Africa Technology Forum, she sums up, "is the soul of the company. It gives us a reason for being beyond making money."

Craigslist.org

Craigslist is by far the smallest and most informal company interviewed for this book. In mid-2003, the company, which provides online classified advertising services in the San Francisco Bay Area and 22 other locations, had 13 employees and was looking for its 14th. In his on-site bio at *www.craigslist.org/about/teambios.html*, the founder, Craig Newmark, describes himself like this:

Craig is a hardcore Java and Web programmer who grew up wearing a plastic pocket protector and thick black glasses, taped together, the full nerd cliché. He started Craigslist in early '95 as a means of better connecting to people by letting them know about cool or useful events happening around San Francisco. It rapidly grew and built a large community of people who wonder if there really is someone named Craig involved with this.

Originally operated out of Newmark's house, Craigslist now has offices in a converted residence near San Francisco's Golden Gate Park. Newmark and CEO Jim Buckmaster share the same space, both working frantically on their computers at the same time as they conducted this interview. Newmark was simultaneously doing customer service and trying to fend off a fanatic who regularly posts to the site. Craigslist's corporate mission is somewhat philanthropic: "giving each other a break, getting the word out about everyday, real-world stuff; restoring the human voice to the Internet, in a humane, non-commercial environment." There are no banner ads on the Website; rather, Craigslist is funded by fees paid by employers to post job openings to the site. Other users, including most nonprofits, pay nothing.

At the same time, Newmark wanted to leverage Craigslist in the philanthropic world. Although the company does not give direct grants, it does have a 501(c)(3) foundation, whose mission is "to bring visibility to small, grassroots nonprofits involved in local social change work, through craigslist.org Websites, community events, and special projects connecting nonprofits and new supporters." It will also match up to 2 percent of an employee's salary in donations to a nonprofit. Like Craigslist itself, the foundation is a very fluid, changing operation, Newmark says. "Most of what we do is spontaneous and organic," born out of a commitment to serve the community that is the company's reason for being in the first place. To that end, it allows nonprofits with less than $1 million in annual income to post job openings for free, actually quite a service, because Craigslist is considered the most effective job site in the San Francisco Bay Area, according to the technology market research firm Forrester Group. Craigslist also hosts about a dozen Websites for nonprofits, such as Women Against Rape in San Francisco and the Henny Street Settlement in New York. Hosting other nonprofits is a service that Newmark would like to expand but hasn't the manpower to do for now. The company also posts schools' and nonprofits' "wish lists" on its site, allowing these organizations to match their needs with what companies are willing to donate, such as computers or other equipment. Says Newmark, "If you're a teacher or staff at a nonprofit or school, you can say why I need this stuff, please buy it for us. The donors get a discount [if the item is for sale on Craigslist] and a tax donation." Teachers in the area have been avid participants in the wish list. Hanging on the wall of Newmark and Buckmaster's joint office is a personal, handmade thank-you note from the kindergartners at Ulloa Elementary School. "Thank you for the wonderful things for our classroom," it says. All the kids' pictures are pasted onto the card, and they've signed their own names. Buckmaster confides that another school sent over chocolate chip cookies once as a thank you, although they're no longer in evidence. Employees may also donate time or money to their own kids' schools; when they give cash, "I just ask the accountant to cut a check and we match it," says Newmark.

Another effort that Craigslist has sponsored is periodic nonprofit venture forums to link up nonprofit organizations with possible funders. The 2003 Nonprofit Funding Competition—promoted on Craigslist with partners including Social Stimulus, Keiretsu Forum Charitable Foundation, Impact Philanthropy LLC, and salesforce.com—awarded $100,000 to social entrepreneurs with financially sustainable, long-term philanthropic initiatives. (The 2003 winners were: Respond Incorporated, which aids battered women and their children through the sale of CDs by well-known artists; Rainn, which operates a national sexual assault online hotline; and MyTwoFrontTeeth.org, which enables online donations of toys to children in need.) Newmark acknowledges that he wants to leverage Craigslist's efforts more on the venture forums. "They may not have generated as much interest in nonprofits as the time and work we put into them would justify," he says. "We've put on about a half dozen venture forums ourselves. I don't know if we'll do more on that basis." Rather, Craigslist will utilize its popular Website to promote such efforts and encourage participation by nonprofits and funders. Newmark puts his finger on a small company's dilemma when he says that Craigslist, which has been expanding rapidly into other cities, including international locations, doesn't have the capacity to do much more in terms of philanthropy.

"There are time and resource constraints," he says. "We're 13 people with 3 million customers. Both Jim and I put in 60-hour weeks, and the first thing to consider is good customer service. We don't want to embarrass ourselves."

Nonetheless, Newmark considers philanthropy to be a high priority for his company and won't give it up. He's just mulling how to do it effectively, along with building Craigslist and keeping customers satisfied. The employees like it, and so does the leadership team. Buckmaster stopped typing on his computer long enough to add that the goal of Craigslist is to be philanthropic on both the for-profit and nonprofit side. His advice to other small companies: "Don't have philanthropy as an afterthought. If you've made tons of ill-gotten gains, don't try to make up for it by giving some as a charitable contribution." As a private corporation, "we do have the flexibility to put public service much higher on our agenda than most companies," he acknowledges.

Propel Software Corporation

Steve Kirsch, the founder and CEO of Propel, is a serial entrepreneur who has founded several other software companies, including Infoseek Corporation (the search engine company acquired by Walt Disney Company) and Frame Technology (acquired by Adobe Systems). In his own right, Kirsch is an active philanthropist, having started a $75-million foundation with his wife Michele. At Propel, which he started in late 1999 to speed up dial-up access to the Internet, he brought the same philosophy of doing philanthropy early in the company's history. Like Craigslist, Propel, which had about 35 employees in mid-2003, began its efforts in a non-cash way at first, through employee volunteerism and in-kind gifts. Kirsch has also endowed a foundation with prepublic stock, 1 percent of Propel's equity, although that has not so far yielded cash for grants. "There really is no way to monetize it yet," says Mary Korn, Propel's chief financial officer and keeper of the stock, "but every investor understands that we have set aside stock for a foundation. The commitment is there." Kirsch points out that potential investors do not regard the presence of the foundation as a negative. Most see it as a positive that will help attract highly qualified employees. "There's always this cachet that goes along with having a foundation," Korn remarks.

Even in the absence of grants, Kirsch has other ideas for how to contribute to the community. For example, "you can use funds that would have been dedicated to a company holiday party to purchase gifts for under-privileged youth," he says. "Each employee could have the opportunity to deliver a gift—in person—to the recipient at a local charitable organization." Echoing what Cisco Systems did when it had to lay off employees, he suggests utilizing employees to work at a nonprofit. "You'll be able to attract a high-caliber employee to a nonprofit that it might not be able to afford on its own," he notes. In regard to setting aside 1 percent of equity for the foundation before the company goes public, Kirsch believes that's best done "as soon as you start the company." That way it can be positioned as a carve-out the founders decided upon before seeking venture capital and other investment. "Since investors would know about the carve-out before they invested, it won't be perceived as 'management using shareholders' money to donate to charity,'" he says. Finally, if a company is paying a cash dividend, "allow shareholders to specify a charity to which the money will be donated." Of course, this applies to public companies that pay dividends, but Kirsch believes Propel will be in those ranks someday. Meanwhile, he is establishing the precedent for philanthropy early.

To date, the main resource for Propel's philanthropy is employee volunteerism. Propel allows employees to take up to 20 hours a year of paid time off to do volunteer work at schools and other nonprofits. "Just creating this opportunity has significant impact on the culture," CFO Korn says. The company also does concerted volunteer work such as food bank drives and a family giving tree, where employees bring a gift for disadvantaged families. Propel executives have gone into local schools as "principal for a day," to learn about the issues facing education and so educators can learn about the issues facing business and technology companies as well. "Part of our philosophy is that work is an extension of the community," she says. "You have to make volunteerism accessible to employees." Another way to aid nonprofits is to allow your facilities to be used for meetings and other activities, Korn adds. She serves on the board of a local nonprofit, Young Audiences, which offers music programs to entice youth and has taken advantage of Propel's facilities on occasion. In fact, Korn says she joined Propel partly because Kirsch and the other executives appreciated the importance of her nonprofit work.

Like most technology companies founded during the Internet boom, today Propel has to function on a much leaner and meaner basis. "We've hit a number of rough patches," Korn says, "but even though we've had to lay people off, we still know that we need to do philanthropy. The employees recognize that we have so much, we have to help others." Besides, she adds, "giving makes you feel good about yourself and the company. It's a win-win; both the community and individual benefit. It makes for a more well-rounded employee who learns about budgeting and strategic planning at a nonprofit and transfers those skills into what he or she does at work." The whole concept behind the corporation is that it survives individuals and becomes a lasting entity, Korn notes. "To do that, you need to understand what's important to your employees and to have a sense of your community."

It's a Small World

Firms employing 500 or fewer people account for more than half of the jobs in the United States, according to 2000 statistics from the U.S. Department of Labor. Firms with fewer than 20 people employ 26 million and those with between 20 and 99 people employ 25 million. And the total number of firms with fewer than 20 people is 5 million, which far dwarfs any other category. Those companies with more than 500 employees, by contrast, total just 17,000. So, even though large companies may be able to afford to give more resources individually, small firms collectively have an important role to play in corporate philanthropy. If small companies decide they aren't big enough to make a difference or that they need to wait to start community service, they're mistaken, and the consequences will have a ripple effect internally and externally. For, as indicated in earlier chapters, if you don't inculcate philanthropy into your culture, it's much more difficult to do later on. Sure, you can give $100 million to a grand project, such as delivering computers to schools, but you won't penetrate into the hearts and minds of employees and, by extension, into the heart and mind of the company itself, as salesforce.com's model has done.

That said, smaller companies have to get real about what they can do in terms of philanthropy. Obviously, big cash gifts are probably out of the question. Business for Social Responsibility's Dinah Waldsmith advises small companies to sit down and decide what they can actually afford to spend on philanthropy. You can do this either on a percentage basis— say, 1 percent of profits or equity—or as a predetermined sum: *We're going to spend $10,000 this year on philanthropy.* Employee time and in-kind giving may be the most valuable contribution that small companies (and even large ones) can make. If you can encourage half of your employees to spend four hours a month at a nonprofit by offering paid time, those hours quickly add up to significant community service. Surveying employees on their own philanthropic interests—and then providing matching dollars for their time or money—builds rapport and loyalty. "Look at the communities where you're located, the markets you're serving, and what their needs are," Waldsmith suggests. "Pick one or two things that you feel the company and employees know about or would like to learn about, and then start small with your philanthropic effort. Don't be afraid to go slow." One of the most disconcerting things for small companies is to plunge in and excitedly announce a grant program, only to get inundated with requests far beyond their ability to handle, which is why it's so important to define a mission prior to opening up the purse strings.

As your program evolves, "reflect on what you're learning and refine your philanthropy plan just the way you would with your business plan," Waldsmith adds. "Come up with what are going to be indicators that you can do more," for example, reaching a certain profit or revenue level. And don't forget there are plenty of resources in the nonprofit sector who will be glad to help you design a program (for more on this, see Chapter 12 on intermediaries). Above all, as Waldsmith says, "You're not in this alone. If you need advice, ask for it."

Maintaining Philanthropy
Through Tough Times

The real measure of a corporation's commitment to philanthropy happens when the company runs into a rough patch: profits are falling or nonexistent, revenues may be shrinking, layoffs are occurring, employees are demoralized, and management is scrambling to meet financial targets. In this kind of scenario, what is the role of philanthropy? If you believe the old saying by economist Milton Friedman—that Corporate America's only interest should be in maximizing profits—then, in difficult times, you might suggest jettisoning philanthropy to cut costs and conserve employee time. But you, along with Friedman, would be wrong. Philanthropy may be even more important to a corporation during these kinds of times as a signal to employees, customers, partners, and other stakeholders that things will get better, and that we're taking a long-term view of the world that includes service to our community. Community service can raise morale—even when business indicators are down—as demonstrated by the employee of Cadence Design Systems, mentioned previously, who wanted to contribute even as she was being escorted out on her last day on the job. That shows that employees who are being laid off recognize that there is a world beyond them, and that many people in their community are far worse off than they are.

"If you assume that you run a company for more than shareholders who have a very narrow interest, then you maintain philanthropy," says

David Vidal, director of research, global corporate citizenship, for The Conference Board. The world today has moved beyond Friedman, he says. "The notion that the role of a corporation is only to satisfy shareholders is nonsense. Consequently, a company's management shouldn't be running a business exclusively in the interest of shareholders." Instead, management must take into account the needs of stakeholders ranging from employees to customers, from advocacy groups to politicians. "Philanthropy—part of being a good corporate citizen—is in the social air the company breathes," he says. Thus, it cannot, and should not, be excised. Susan Colby, a partner with the Bridgespan Group, concedes that the inclination, when earnings are dropping, is to go after philanthropy—often a juicy target with high-dollar contributions. That's why she advises many clients to undertake smaller projects that can exist under the radar of financial scrutiny—things like funding a day-care center or supplying books to a community center. It's not unfair to expect the philanthropic budget to take its lumps along with other cost centers, Colby adds, "but you don't want to just cut willy-nilly if you can help it," because that sends a message of desperation and panic.

Even companies whose philanthropic endeavors are run out of an endowed foundation can have trouble in difficult economic times. Many foundations are "endowed" with stock from the parent company, so their holdings may decline in value as the company suffers. At the Salesforce.com Foundation, we sell any donated stock immediately and place the money in more stable financial instruments. Meanwhile, foundations or corporate giving programs that receive a certain percentage of earnings—typically, 1 percent—are also at risk. If you're not making any money, 1 percent of nothing is nothing. So some companies that are committed to philanthropy will establish a baseline for what they give, exceeding that baseline in good years so that they can sock away money in the foundation to cover bad years. At the same time, they're cautious about committing to too many projects that require multiyear funding and that indicate to grant recipients that they should make sure to diversify their revenue sources. In this chapter, we take a look at a regulated utility, Pacific Gas & Electric Company, which had to cut philanthropic giving entirely after it filed for Chapter 11 bankruptcy protection and is now slowly ramping up again. We also profile Autodesk, which decided it had to eliminate its foundation, but found alternative ways to incorporate much of its giving; Levi Strauss, which closed plants and laid off workers around the world, then used foundation funding to give them retraining grants; and a small company, AppsTech, which also kept its global philanthropy going despite severe business challenges.

Pacific Gas & Electric Company

PG&E, the San Francisco-based gas and electric utility that serves most of Northern California, filed for bankruptcy in April 2001 as a result of the energy crisis that roiled California in 2000–2001, creating supply shortages and driving up prices. Several out-of-state energy producers, including the infamous Enron, were sued by California for allegedly manipulating the market. PG&E's bankruptcy filing was controversial in that it included only the utility company itself and not the corporate parent. Critics charged that the utility was trying to escape responsibility for its own errors in the massive energy crisis. With its reputation in shreds, PG&E also faced the added burden of figuring out what to do with its corporate giving program, which had amounted to $7–$9 million annually before the Chapter 11 filing. Larry Goldzband had only recently joined PG&E as manager of its Charitable Contributions Department, which handles the utility's giving. The parent, PG&E Corporation, has a separate foundation. To Goldzband fell the unenviable task of cutting philanthropy back to nothing for a short time; and then gradually reviving it on a different basis. "I joined the company in October 1999," he says, "and a year later we were out of business as far as grantmaking." As PG&E took steps such as suspending its dividend to shareholders, management felt compelled to shut down the grantmaking, telling Goldzband of the decision in late 2000. "We're not giving a dividend to our shareholders and yet we have a charitable contributions program? How could we justify that?" he says. As a regulated utility, PG&E also had to consider how ratepayers would feel about seeing their bills increase while the company handed out millions to nonprofits.

The PG&E corporate foundation picked up some of the slack. In 2001 it contributed around $1 million; in 2002, $3.3 million. In 2003, PG&E Company took back the program, putting in $3.3 million. Still, that represented only 38 percent of the previous level. Goldzband says the decision to continue giving, even on a very limited basis, was made out of concern for further damage to PG&E's reputation. After all, what is more of a community company than the local utility? "We were worried about all the bad press we would get if we were spending money on grants," says Goldzband. But there was also concern about the impact on the community and on PG&E's standing in it if giving were shut down entirely. "You see it from both sides," he says. "For a nonprofit, when a major employer like PG&E goes down, it's horrible." Through the bankruptcy process, PG&E did make sure that nonprofits to whom it had already promised grants received their checks; San Francisco's Asian Art Museum, in the process of renovating a new location, got the $100,000 PG&E had committed, for example. Goldzband points out that contributions by the utility all come from shareholder dollars, not ratepayers. "It's tremendously important that we're out in the community making philanthropic donations," he says, adding that PG&E's chief executive and chief financial officer both sit on nonprofit boards and knew the pain they were causing by cutting back on grants. At the same time, "we recognize the value of maintaining these relationships the best we can," Goldzband says.

To exercise damage control, Goldzband's department sent out letters explaining the situation to every single grant recipient who had to be cut off from future donations. "We were all terribly concerned about not being as involved with the community, but we were hemorrhaging dollars due to a dysfunctional regulatory system," he says. "We had to save our company." Nonprofits that lost funding ranged from United Way to the National Fish and Wildlife Foundation; United Way giving by PG&E dropped from $1.7 million (excluding employee donations) to around $200,000. On a limited basis, using the parent foundation's $1 million, PG&E made a few very targeted donations in 2001. One was to give money to food banks, reeling from the skyrocketing energy costs, to buy energy-efficient equipment such as refrigerators and stoves. "That was a great win," Goldzband enthuses. "There was a clear community need, the giving supports our business goals, and we got good press," something that beleaguered PG&E could really use. The funds that still go to United Way are more tightly focused than before. "We decided to give $140,000 to United Way of the Bay Area for its Safe Communities program, which includes emergency preparedness," says Goldzband, allowing PG&E to leverage its experience and relationships in that area. "We're cobranding with United Way on cards listing what you need in an emergency." The cards state: "PG&E and United Way are doing this to keep your community safe."

As charitable giving increased to $3.3 million in both 2002 and 2003, PG&E revamped its philanthropic program. "When you have less than 40 percent of your original budget, you still have to cut and cut away," he points out. Previously, PG&E's giving was around the industry benchmark, a half percent of pretax profits, Goldzband says. At $3.3 million, "we're between one-third and one-half of the benchmark." The mission for philanthropy remains threefold: fulfilling a community need in PG&E's service area, addressing the company's near-term business goals, and being able to communicate the participation in positive fashion with local news media. Historically, says Goldzband, "we have done education, the environment, and community development." After filing for Chapter 11, PG&E moved in the opposite direction of many corporations by becoming more reactive rather than proactive on its philanthropy. "We decided that if somebody's got a good project out there, we'll consider it," says Goldzband. Not only that, PG&E will do what many corporations won't—provide money for general operating expenses, which makes nonprofits ecstatic. (For the nonprofit view, see Chapter 14.) "Between the economic recession and 9/11, nonprofits in our service area are in trouble," he adds. "We'll look at the community as a whole and give funds where they're needed the most. It doesn't have to be programmatic. We'll say we're more than happy to be associated with you. If [operating expenses] is what you need the money for, that's fine."

As a regulated utility, PG&E cannot give away free electricity or natural gas, but it does donate other types of equipment, such as surplus vehicles or pipe. For example, it donated a large amount of pipe to Ducks Unlimited in the Sacramento Valley for habitat restoration. It also gave used vehicles to fire departments around the state. And, with thousands of employees accustomed to emergency work, PG&E encourages volunteerism, although it does not have a paid time-off policy. "We're revisiting that issue," says Goldzband. "It has to do with who pays for the time off, shareholder versus ratepayer funding." Meanwhile, executives and employees have ample opportunities for using their own time, particularly to "take environmental stewardship throughout our territory." For instance, on a recent Saturday, hundreds of PG&E volunteers helped spruce up eight parks in the state; the company donated $50,000 for habitat restoration. PG&E also invited retirees and local public officials to join in the effort. As PG&E recovers from bankruptcy and seeks to restore its reputation with customers and others, philanthropy will play an important role, Goldzband believes. "The only way to rebuild a reputation is over a sustained time base, investing in communities, and making sure we have good relationships with people we can trust to give us information on community needs."

Autodesk Incorporated

Autodesk, founded in 1982 in Marin County north of San Francisco, seized the lead in one of the early niches of the technology revolution: computer-aided design (CAD) software used by everyone from architects to automotive designers. The company also had another notable first when it recruited Carol Bartz, a former executive at Sun Microsystems and Digital Equipment Corporation, to be its CEO in 1992. Bartz was the first woman brought in from the outside to head a major technology company. Both Autodesk founder John Walker and Bartz were strong proponents of education. "Autodesk has a real passion for education in general," Bartz says. Reflecting her views, Autodesk, like many technology companies, centered its philanthropic efforts there. Then, training students at universities and high schools to use Autodesk's primary product, Autocad, proved to have business advantages as well. They tended to want to use the same program when they joined the working world. "The founders [of Autodesk] were very generous in giving software away and establishing relationships with schools," recalls Alice Ostrovsky, Autodesk's manager of workforce development programs. "It was tied to a strategy for growing the original Autocad business." Out of that effort came the decision to establish an educational foundation that was designed to support educators in teaching technology in 1990. The goal was to partner with schools "to develop improvements in education so that kids are better prepared for life and work in the information age," Bartz says. "That means shifting the emphasis from just teachers talking about things to students actually doing things, and making sure our schools are not isolated from the rest of our communities."[1]

The foundation was unusual, however, in that its primary resource wasn't money, but Autodesk employees. "Our best resource was our people," says Ostrovsky. "The foundation was about connecting teachers with our employee base, not about making grants." At its height, the foundation had a staff of eight people, utilizing educators as visiting experts. It would develop software, in partnership with third parties, on project-based learning. The foundation then brought in teachers from around the country to train them in using the software, with employees providing the instruction. But in 1998, not long after Ostrovsky joined Autodesk, the company hit the wall. "We went through a 10-percent reduction in workforce across the board that fall," she remembers. At that point, "given the economic and employment climate of having to reduce our workforce for the first time ever, the justification was not there to continue this large educational reform organization." The foundation was eliminated, with its work in education reform spun out to other foundations, such as Connect, based in Boston. One portion of the foundation's work, the school-to-career program, which brought high school interns into Autodesk for training, was integrated into human resources under Ostrovsky.

The school-to-career program, operated under a corporate, cross-departmental initiative called Design Your Future, was the brainchild of CEO Bartz. She was particularly concerned about the male-female gap in science and math, and wanted to assign mentors at Autodesk to work with young women in finding opportunities for themselves in the technology world. After Autodesk closed its foundation, "we decided to put the internship program within Design Your Future," says Ostrovsky. "Because we were able to demonstrate that this was about workforce development and not just about PR, we could show a benefit and get the program funded." She adds, "It's not just about giving grants to the community, it's about attracting the best and brightest to Autodesk." With an annual budget of around $235,000, Ostrovsky brings Autodesk resources to local schools, and also puts high school interns to work throughout the company. Each year Autodesk selects a school district and a nonprofit organization to partner with in bringing science and math to girls. In 2003, it worked with the National Science Foundation and Oakland Public Middle Schools in training girls in technology, including helping them gain access to a computer lab. A separate program, called I-mentoring, has matched 45 women at Autodesk with girls, who can e-mail their mentors with questions about the workforce, personal development, and the like.

Ostrovsky says what the Design Your Future and intern programs show is that it's not necessary to have a foundation or make significant grants to have an impactful program. "The staying power of Design Your Future is partially due to executive sponsorship," she says. "We have a CEO who believes in volunteerism. The motivation is that this is where the future talent is, and we want to grow a workforce early. That helps us have staying power when dollars get examined." Ostrovsky says the 100 or so interns whom Autodesk is employing are doing real work at the company, contributing to software development teams, doing quality assessment, and establishing media contacts. And the company winds up hiring between 2 and 5 percent of its interns. Even though Autodesk has had to tighten its charitable donations budget, "we try to do more and more with our people and less with dollars," she says.

Autodesk also has a charitable giving program within the corporation, run by Julie Wilder, community relations manager. Her budget for the past two years has been $500,000 annually, both to make donations and provide matching funds for employee gifts to nonprofits. Donations go into five categories: arts and culture, civic and community, education, environment, and health and human services. More than half of the funding goes to the latter category, helping low-income families, the elderly, and the disabled, Wilder says. Autodesk also continues to give away software through Gifts In Kind, a nonprofit that distributes technology. "We cannot be all things to all people, and we have to say no," she says. "That's the hardest part of my job. We donate where Autodesk has a physical presence, including overseas." She tends to respond primarily to "real human needs," people who are hungry or need equipment to enable them to do daily activities. Recently, for example, Autodesk gave nearby Point Reyes National Seashore a grant to buy an all-terrain wheelchair so that disabled people can enjoy the beach there. Wilder says she enlists employees to be "team leaders" on various community service projects, such as the AIDS Walk or Run for the Seals. Designating these team leaders gives employees recognition and also helps Wilder leverage her time. "People direct their questions to the team leaders," she says. Once a year, there's a catered lunch recognizing employee volunteers at which Bartz speaks. Employees can take four hours a month of paid time to volunteer by clearing the time with their manager. Echoing Ostrovsky, she says that community service at Autodesk depends heavily on its people, especially as actual dollars get cut in line with other budgets at the company.

Levi Strauss & Co.

The apparel maker Levi Strauss celebrated its 150th anniversary on May 1, 2003. Its philanthropic tradition is nearly as long-lived. Founder Levi Strauss, a Bavarian immigrant to San Francisco, donated $5 (the equivalent of $100 today) to a local orphanage shortly after arriving in 1853. Consequently, even as it was forced to close plants worldwide and lay off thousands of workers in the late 1990s, Levi continued to fund its foundation, which established special programs in areas affected by layoffs. When the Levi Strauss Foundation got started in 1952, "the company immediately started building a reserve," says Theresa Fay-Bustillos, executive director of the foundation. A privately held company, Levi didn't endow its foundation with stock, nor does it take outside donations. "It's only what the company gives us," she says. "The philosophy is that we're going to give you this in good times, and you build a reserve against bad times." She adds, "When you've been here for 150 years, you understand that business is cyclical. In spite of sound business strategies, it's hard to avoid those bad times." Another reason for building the reserve—and avoiding outside contributions—is to allow the foundation "to continue to operate in our courageous, risk-taking, impactful way." Levi's goal is nothing less than fighting poverty on a worldwide basis, by focusing on preventing the spread of HIV and AIDS and providing economic development and educational opportunities to socially disadvantaged women and youth. In 1982, it was the first corporation to address the new disease sweeping through populations in its headquarter city, as well as other areas of the country, by handing out informational pamphlets and funding a clinic.

Fay-Bustillos explains that both the company and the foundation contribute directly to communities. The company has donated, annually, about $3 million to communities in the last few years—far below what it previously gave, but still significant. "Our benchmark is 2.5 percent of pretax earnings, for direct corporate giving to communities and for the foundation to build its reserve," she says. The foundation, with $70 million in assets, has been giving around $10–12 million a year, down from its peak of $20 million in the late 1990s. Still, if you do the math, taking out $10–12 million means you draw down on your assets pretty severely. At its height, again in the late 1990s after the stock market boom, the foundation had assets of $119 million. Since the downturn began in 1997, Levi has been reaching into its reserve, with the expectation that sooner or later the economy will improve and the company's profitability will return. But, like her peers, Fay-Bustillos says the commitment to philanthropy is especially important in tough times. "When we talk to our employees who are getting laid off, they still feel that this was a great company to work for, in part, because of everything we do in the community," she says. "We want to maintain that perspective."

Demonstrating its continuing commitment, the foundation partnered with its sister foundation at the company—the Red Tab Foundation—and launched innovative economic development programs to give grants, for two years, in communities where it closed its owned or operated plants. (Since 1997, Levi has closed 38 plants around the world in which nearly 20,000 people were employed.) The grants can go toward emergency assistance for workers in danger of losing their homes or at risk in other ways. The monies, administered through local nonprofits, also go to creating new jobs and enabling workers to go back to school or start small businesses of their own. "The goal we have is to build the capacity of these communities to meet the needs of laid-off workers," says Fay-Bustillos. "People have told us, you can't take employees with an eighth-grade education and limited English skills and have them start businesses," she recalls. But based on surveys that Levi did in communities where it closed plants, there was tremendous interest in starting small businesses, she adds. Many of the communities had been affected by other plant closings as well. "We would fund agencies that take these workers with entrepreneurial instincts and teach them how to start their own microbusinesses. Before we started funding this, people didn't believe it would work here."

Fay-Bustillos says Levi has had to cut some nonprofits off from its funding due to $10 million lost to declining budgets. "Many of our grants are one-year grants," she notes, so the nonprofits don't expect to be funded over a number of years. Then too, the Levi Foundation, which puts a lot of emphasis on long-range planning, will assess the capacity-building ability and sustainability of the agencies that it funds. "We will give them general support funds to build that up," she says. "If we think someone is doing great work, we will help them build their capacity to do more of it. If that means giving behind-the-scenes grants to fund administration and support, we will do that," she says. These capacity-building grants are something that many corporate philanthropy programs don't do, because they're more interested in projects.

AppsTech

AppsTech, the private technology company introduced in Chapter 4, wasn't immune to the technology downturn that hit hard in 2001. Its partners, such as Oracle, were also hurting, and revenues for AppsTech were falling. Founder and CEO Rebecca Enonchong called a companywide meeting to talk about how to cut expenses. To her relief, "not one person suggested we cut our investment in the Africa Technology Forum," the largely AppsTech-funded philanthropic organization that seeks to promote technology entrepreneurialism in Africa. "It's such a part of this company that it never occurred to anyone." Instead, the employees suggested cutting back on their health insurance, eliminating their cell phone perk, and even taking a salary cut, if that's what it took. The two full-time employees who run the Forum stepped up to the plate along with everyone else. "Some of the employees came in and said, 'I can go without pay for several months.' People are willing to sacrifice to help their colleagues so that nobody gets laid off, including the Africa Tech Forum folks," she says. Enonchong managed to avoid layoffs and salary cuts. "We did do delays in the payment of salaries," she says, but the Forum continued. "It's an important part of the culture," she says, "showing that we're all in this together," including the philanthropic arm of the company.

Enonchong concedes that if she had had venture capital funding or other formal investors, she might have had a more difficult time saving the Africa Technology Forum and its annual budget of about $500,000, most of which comes from AppsTech. That makes a very appealing target when the company's survival is at stake, especially to investors who may not be wedded to the same philanthropic ideals. Fortunately, "we're a bootstrapped company," she says, meaning that the money behind the company comes from herself and close friends and family. Although that approach "makes it hard sometimes" because of the limits on investment, at the same time, "you can make your own decisions about your culture," she says. "The flexibility has made a huge difference. With bank financing or venture funding, we would not be able to do these things."

She believes that AppsTech's emphasis on philanthropy enhances team spirit and will help the company be a survivor. Since its founding, AppsTech has had no voluntary turnover, Enonchong stresses. "Absolutely philanthropy is part of that," she says. "People are not just coming here to make money. They're interested in doing something very positive, in making a difference." Much more than stock options—AppsTech has not yet implemented a stock option plan—the Africa Technology Forum "helps us with retention," even with employees who are not of African background. Employees know coming in that the Forum is a part of what AppsTech does, so the company attracts the kind of people interested in the so-called "triple bottom line," which refers to making profits, having good customer relationships, and serving the community. "I've told [would-be] venture capital investors that if you look at the companies you've funded without this kind of culture, where are they today?" she says. "The way you treat your communities and your stakeholders is just as important as making money."

Philanthropy as a Higher Need

Anyone who has ever taken a high school or college psychology course has probably become acquainted with Abraham Maslow's Hierarchy of Needs, which holds that once human beings satisfy the very basic requirements of food, shelter, and the like, they move up the pyramid to "higher" needs such as love, esteem, and self-actualization. Enlightened companies today recognize that their employees, first of all, want to be able to provide adequately for themselves and their families. But beyond that, they are interested in reaching out to their communities, in giving back. This motivation used to be satisfied through donations to formal religious organizations, but today corporate and community groups are stepping into that role. This means that, at companies such as AppsTech, philanthropy can be a mechanism for uniting people behind a cause, like the Africa Technology Forum. At companies such as PG&E, Levi, and Autodesk, philanthropy can provide employees and executives with a much-needed source of pride, particularly in difficult times.

The budget devoted to community giving can seem a logical place to cut when a corporation is suffering through declining revenues and profits, layoffs, and other problems. To be sure, philanthropic giving has to be subject to the same budget constraints that affect other departments, so that, say, a 10 percent across-the-board cut does apply to philanthropic donations. Smart nonprofits realize that corporate giving programs and foundations are buffeted by the same economic ill winds that affect any other group, so they diversify and don't become dependent on just a handful of donors. Likewise, corporations work with their nonprofit partners to make sure that other funding sources are available, as Autodesk did when it closed its educational foundation. If at all possible, corporations for whom community involvement becomes a part of the culture do not eliminate philanthropy in bad years. They may cut back on cash donations, as PG&E did; they may close foundations, as Autodesk did; they may shift priorities, as Levi Strauss did. But they keep intact the spirit of giving by leveraging other resources, including employee volunteerism and expertise. That sends an important signal that this company stands for long-term values, not only to the outside world, but to employees as well. Such a signal can shore up morale and help employees believe that there are better times ahead.

The 1-Percent Solution

These are my experiences and thoughts as the CEO of salesforce.com. In February of 2001, I joined 3,000 other chief executives at the World Economic Forum (WEF) in New York City to discuss the nature of globalization and the consequences that it has on local economies, welfare, and the environment. While few would dispute the economic benefits that large corporations bring to the international marketplace, there has yet to emerge a clear consensus on what it means for a corporation to be part of the global economy, what responsibilities this role brings with it, or the best way to fulfill those obligations.

This uncertainty has bred suspicion among those on the receiving end of globalization and inspired fierce protests wherever the world's economic and financial leaders meet—opposition that often falls on deaf ears. While 10,000 protesters lined the streets outside the WEF, presenter Zaki Laïdi, a senior research fellow at France's Centre d'Etudes et de Researches Internationales, put the problem succinctly: "Globalization is not providing a collective purpose. There is a lack of tolerance for an alternative perspective."

Still, even the world's richest man can see the validity of the protests. Microsoft Chairman Bill Gates, presenting at the WEF, said, "It's a healthy thing that there are demonstrators in the streets. We need a discussion about whether the rich world is giving back what it should to the developing world. I think there is a legitimate question whether we are." Gates has backed up his words by becoming the world's largest philanthropist since endowing the Bill and Melinda Gates Foundation with $24 billion in January 2000. Engaged in a highly focused effort to combat some of the developing world's most serious illnesses, such as HIV/AIDS, the foundation is led by one of Gates's former top lieutenants from Microsoft, Patty Stonesifer. The foundation represents one of the most significant acts ever, from a captain of corporate industry—an inspiration for all entrepreneurs, big and small.

Who would criticize this incredible act of charity? But imagine: What if this had been started 25 years ago, upon Microsoft's founding, rather than at the culmination of a lifetime's achievement? What if Gates also donated 1 percent of his employees' time to the communities they serve, unleashing a true "army of compassion" of tens of thousands of smart, capable people around the world? What if Gates were able to lead the foundation from within Microsoft as a key corporate function? How could his company use its relationships with the world's largest corporations to advance other social causes?

But the Gates Foundation remains a family endeavor, separate from Microsoft's own corporate philanthropy. Microsoft and many companies are struggling to define what role they should play in giving back to the community. Nearly all agree that philanthropy is desirable, but the key question is: How can corporations move beyond isolated acts of philanthropy to more fully integrate corporate responsibility into the new global system?

The Disenfranchised Globalized Corporation

The protestors in New York and the attendees of the World Social Forum held concurrently in Porto Alegre, Brazil, feel that globalization is destroying the native cultures, economies, and environments of the poor, undeveloped, and unrepresented billions. They believe that heedless of the social and physical environment, globalization is fostering the creation of a new global consciousness based on pure capitalism alone. Sadly, this view is supported by numerous examples of corporations acting without a sense of corporate responsibility, from child labor and sweatshop practices to deforestation to job displacement and relocation. In a business culture that values the generation of profits for shareholders above all else, the typical globalized corporation is completely disenfranchised from the communities in which it operates.

In previous generations of business, it was a different story. Local businesses served local communities, and their value stayed in the community. Profits were reinvested locally, and business owners heard and responded to local feedback. As corporations prospered and grew, stakeholders throughout the community—not merely the stockholders who owned the company—shared in the rise. The system was hardly perfect, but it was far more equitable than under today's globalized corporations.

Consider McDonald's, a poster child for the rapidly expanding globalized brand—and a favorite target for protesters. As the company moves into new markets, it replaces local establishments owned by community stakeholders with corporate-owned stores staffed with minimum-wage workers. Profits and equity are returned to corporate headquarters, rather than to the local economy, formerly supported by the businesses it has displaced. To be sure, McDonald's has done a lot on the philanthropic front, particularly for children with cancer, but does that adequately compensate for the cultural homogenization and loss of community identity that its presence can cause in global markets?

The End of Philanthropy

No business should remain at odds with its community, whether that community is a small town or the entire world. The fundamental questions facing today's modern corporations are: How can we address the valid issues raised by the protesters while still doing business? How can we establish that the corporation is not disenfranchised from its community, but a vital member? How can we develop a model that integrates a commitment to all our stakeholders, not solely to our shareholders? How can we accomplish all this while preserving the concept and the economic benefits of a globalized corporation?

Businesses often turn to corporate philanthropy as a way to demonstrate their goodwill toward society, while serving the greater good. In 1997, while I was still at Oracle Corporation, Colin Powell stood up with the five living presidents and launched America's Promise, motivating CEO Larry Ellison's decision to start Oracle's Promise. Larry asked me to oversee the program, which did succeed in placing thousands of computers, training, and curriculum in hundreds of schools worldwide in less than two years.

Fulfilling Oracle's Promise

In 1997, the CEO of Oracle Corporation, Larry Ellison, responded to then-President George H.W. Bush's challenge to American companies to serve their communities. Bush charged Colin Powell with overseeing that effort, America's Promise. Ellison tapped me, as one of his executives, and told me I had $100 million to deliver computers to schools under Oracle's Promise. The experience was a defining moment that helped launch my concept of integrated philanthropy, now put into practice at salesforce.com.

Jim Cavalieri and Mitch Wallace, both formerly with Oracle's Promise and now with salesforce.com, recall that there was a lot of sheer physical labor involved in bringing thousands of computers to hundreds of schools. In August 1998, Cavalieri, now chief information officer of salesforce.com, was sweating in "ridiculously hot" temperatures and looking up three flights of stairs to where he was supposed to wire up 100 computers for McFarland Middle School in Washington, D.C. The school had about 2,000 students, and Oracle was donating 100 computers for a new lab. He called Powell's office looking for backup, and he dispatched a troop of Marines to the school to carry the computers up the steps. "Then we used America's Promise red wagons to haul them around on the floors," Cavalieri says. "A hundred computers is a lot to set up in one afternoon." In another neighborhood in Chicago, Oracle brought 25 computers each for 10 schools. "The parents were so excited, they made T-shirts for us."

Wallace, now the vice president of business systems for salesforce.com, remembers that in the first Oracle's

Promise project, involving several schools in south central Los Angeles, he and Cavalieri were crawling around schoolrooms "drilling holes and stringing wires." In that first year, Oracle's Promise placed 6,000 computers in schools. "But we had infrastructure issues," Wallace adds. Just getting computers to schools wasn't enough. "Making them work is a much larger challenge." The Oracle's Promise team eventually shot a video showing how to assemble the computers and shipped that along with all the other equipment, such as electrical devices, that would be needed to get the computers up and running. "We couldn't hire people at every school to put the computers together," he says. "We had to figure out, how do you make this fairly complex process simple?"

Oracle's Promise eventually got some help from company employees. "We sent out a corporate-wide e-mail (with the school locations) telling people all they had to do was show up," says Wallace. "We got a lot of response. People were very enthusiastic about helping because they hadn't had that many opportunities." There was a pent-up demand for the chance to do good.

However, the lesson learned, says Cavalieri, is that even though Oracle's Promise was "an awesome program," the small team shepherding it felt "very isolated." He adds, "It was our mission but nobody else's. We weren't able to harness the power of Oracle Corporation in its fullest sense. We got the feeling that if we really were able to leverage a corporation's full assets, what couldn't we accomplish?"

Leveraging all of a corporation's assets to serve the community is what we're trying to accomplish today at salesforce.com.

—Marc Benioff

· · · · · · · · · · · · · · · · · · 🌐

What we learned from Oracle's Promise was that it was possible to make a difference as a company. But we also learned that you would make an even bigger difference if you could leverage all the company's assets, its employees, its customers, and its partners. Michael Milken once said that you have to deliver the full package to be successful in a school: software, hardware, training support, and maintenance. A lot of people just dump computers in schools. With Oracle's Promise, we'd go to schools and find computers hidden away in closets and storage rooms.

When I started salesforce.com two years after leading Oracle's Promise, I hired a lot of people who came from Oracle. We realized that the way to do philanthropy is to build it into the company's culture, to make it "not optional." This is a significant part of the operation of our business at salesforce.com: not only is it key to serve our customers and stakeholders but also to serve the community. With Oracle's Promise, our group was embedded at Oracle, but it wasn't integrated into the culture or the leadership. It's not that we couldn't do the work or that the work wasn't high quality. But we shouldn't have had to put such a huge amount of duress on people to get them to participate. If this had been integrated, they would have realized this is part of what we do.

At the same time, the Oracle's Promise venture was successful enough that it led me to ask a fundamental question: Is there a better way to leverage a global corporation's assets for good than charity in a silo? The problem is that such acts of goodwill happen in isolation, separate from the forces that created them, and are the exception rather than the rule. What is needed is a new architecture for globalization, developed with full awareness of the constraints of the current system— what *Fortune* magazine's David Kirkpatrick, summarizing the work of a small group of social entrepreneurs and new age corporate leaders, has called "The End of Philanthropy," at least as it used to be practiced in stand-alone fashion.

I often ask my peers in Silicon Valley, "What if Sequoia Capital, Kleiner Perkins, or a similar high-quality venture capital firm, required the companies it invested in to put 1 percent of their equity into a public charity serving the communities in which they do business?" The answer is that Cisco, Oracle, Yahoo, and numerous other successful Silicon Valley companies would have built up some of the largest public charities in the world, amassing billions of dollars to help fund multidimensional solutions to the very problems the WEF protesters have cited. This simple idea points to a powerful new way to make *doing good* an integral part of doing business.

The Integrated Corporation

The integrated corporation creates value for shareholders and stakeholders alike. Its size and the location of its headquarters do not dictate a centralized return on its value; rather, its value is fully distributed, not only to its leadership, but to the communities in which it operates, and to the global community as a whole. It is a new architecture for globalization.

Past Model	Present Model	Future Model
Proprietors	Shareholders	Stakeholders
Local Supporters	Global Protestors	Corporate Advocates
Charities	Corporate Philanthropy	Integrated Corporation

Under this architecture, globalized corporations can leverage employees, equity, products, alliances, and relationships to support stakeholders in a way that smaller, local companies could not, demonstrating the company's value to the community, while turning protestors into advocates. But it will take leadership, creativity, innovation, and the investment of resources to make this vision a reality.

A CEO can look at his or her corporation and ask, "Where do I have the most leverage to serve?" Four areas come immediately to mind: corporate value, profits and products, employee time, and government influence. Accordingly, four models have emerged:

1. Place a percentage of corporate equity into a public charity.

2. Return a percentage of profits to the global communities served.

3. Encourage a percentage of employee time to be used for community service activities.

4. Use influence with governments to positively affect policies for global communities.

Forward-looking companies have already implemented these models, validating the concept while demonstrating the dramatic results this new architecture of globalization can achieve. In the integrated corporation, successful philanthropy is organic. It meets community needs, responds quickly, partners with other organizations, and is driven by employees. Almost no one has done all of this, which is why the integrated model is unique.

A Percentage of Equity

When I launched salesforce.com, we also created another legal entity as well: the salesforce.com Foundation, a 501(c)(3) public charity, independently financed, with the mission to provide technology access and media to youth in underserved areas within the communities that salesforce.com serves. Alongside private funding sources, salesforce.com placed more than 1 percent of the new corporation's stock into this foundation. The dream has been that, as the company grows, the foundation will grow proportionately and be fully integrated into the company by which it is powered.

Since its launch in July 2000, the salesforce.com Foundation has built 20 technology centers in San Francisco, two mobile computer labs in Hawaii, and 63 centers in 12 countries internationally. The foundation also encouraged our own employees to donate their personal time to these projects, resulting, thus far, in 10,000 hours of community service donated to the local community. In serving more than 50,000 youths and adults worldwide, the foundation has leveraged the corporation's relationships with AOL Time Warner, Gateway, Cisco, Hewlett-Packard, and other global companies to provide many of the technical and social pieces beyond its own resources. Salesforce.com also provides its online software, without charge, to more than 250 charities, non-governmental organizations (NGOs), and universities worldwide, accounting for approximately 1 percent of our users.

The impact on both our employees and the communities we serve has been highly enriching for all involved. One IT staffer spends his Mondays at a salesforce.com Foundation technology lab, sharing his professional skills with the local youths he mentors. A volunteer from sales support gives time to a tutoring program, providing needed support, positive influence, and communication to an at-risk student. The vice president of marketing works with adults of all ages, with no previous computer experience, helping them add skills to land a new job or prepare professional-looking marketing materials for their small businesses. Meanwhile, groups from the foundation centers regularly visit the salesforce.com offices for Career Days, with some even signing on as intern, to help with everything from finance to marketing to sales. By providing our employees with a vehicle for volunteerism, we help them make community involvement a central part of their lives, just as it forms a core part of our company's operations.

Our initial stock grant should be worth $25–$30 million when we go public. Employees are also making donations of stock to the foundation. About 50 percent of the employees made stock or cash contributions last year and we also get donations from outside individuals. My personal goal is to raise $100–200 million for the foundation over the next five years, in cash and equity contributions.

A Percentage of Profits

As an independent company, Ben & Jerry's took the idea of integrated service furthest of all, fully integrating philanthropy into its products, marketing, and human resource practices. Giving away 7.5 percent of its pretax earnings, Ben & Jerry's funded community service in three ways: through the Ben & Jerry's Foundation, through employee Community Action Teams at five Vermont sites, and through corporate grants made by the director of social mission development. No other company had such an explicit program for donating profits and time. The foundation, managed by a nine-member employee board, looked at proposals relating to children and families, disadvantaged groups, and the environment. (When Unilever took over Ben & Jerry's in 2000, it pledged to continue the programs, but activist groups were skeptical that would happen.)

Merck & Co. is one of the most successful pharmaceutical companies in the world today, generating profits through proprietary designs on many of the world's most important drugs. Several years ago it decided to donate Mectizan, one of its premier products, and the key to controlling river blindness, to African villages. Working with the World Health Organization, the World Bank, dozens of NGOs, and local ministries, Merck provides a valuable resource to an estimated 30 million people annually. This donation of a product and the profit that goes with it has a global impact on social health.

Research verifies time and again that companies can make a major difference with relatively small investments. In tandem with the United Nations, the world's salt manufacturers have made sure that all salt manufactured for human consumption contains iodine. As a result, newborn children are protected against iodine deficiency, a major cause of mental retardation.

At salesforce.com, we've set our benchmark at donating 1 percent of profits to our foundation. That money is disbursed according to goals established by the board of directors of the foundation, along with input from an employee committee. We will continue to donate both cash and equity to the foundation as it grows into a substantial presence in philanthropy.

A Percentage of Time

Alan Hassenfeld, the chairman and then-CEO of Hasbro, attended the World Economic Forum to see how far corporations have come in doing social work. Hassenfeld, who stepped down as CEO in mid-2003, has truly pioneered many of the concepts of the integrated corporation (see Chapter 1). One of his goals is to have 1 percent of corporate time available for service to local communities. His Team Hasbro program serves its communities not only with a corporate foundation, but also with a mission to "Make Our Community Smile." He offers employees four hours of paid time off per month to volunteer with children. They simply log onto the company's Website, which is both a resource for employees and a posting site for nonprofit agencies to announce needs.

Timberland, one of the world's largest outdoor apparel companies, provides another excellent example of volunteerism (see Chapters 1 and 11). In 1992, the company created the Path of Service program, dedicating 16 hours of paid service for each employee to serve the community he or she came from. Just five years later, the program's success led it to be expanded to 40 hours donated per employee. The fully integrated program has now grown to give more than 200,000 hours of service, through more than 200 social service agencies in communities, in 73 American cities, spanning 30 states, as well as in 18 foreign countries.

These examples inspired me to allow the salesforce.com employees to spend 1 percent of their time volunteering, either on their own or as part of company efforts. Suzanne DiBianca, the head of our foundation, is charged with developing relationships with nonprofits to which our employees can make a contribution, including serving at homeless shelters, mentoring children at local schools in technology and media programs, and bringing teenagers to salesforce.com to see what opportunities there are in the technology workforce, among many others.

The True Goal

Through the development of an integrated corporation, the leaders and people within the company will themselves be transformed. Former President Clinton said, "The only path through today's global problems is a higher consciousness." However, it is not enough to speak on it, pray on it, or write about it. We have to do the work and convert our rhetoric into practice as corporate leaders seeking to transform the world. As leaders, we will become integrated, and we will bring that commitment back to our organizations and reflect it throughout.

UN Secretary General Kofi Anan has said, "Those who have the power and means, governments and businesses, must show that economics, properly applied, and profits, wisely invested, can bring social benefits within reach not only for the few, but for the many, and eventually for all." Helping others through a corporate structure returns untold benefits to the corporation, including raising employee morale and aiding in retention. But it cannot be done for that reason alone. It has to be done because it is the right thing to do. It is more than an obligation. It is our responsibility.

While we will be able to clearly measure the benefit of programs like these on society, we should also be conscious of the effect it will have on the organizations providing the service. Employees seeking greater levels of fulfillment in their own lives will have to look no further than their workplace. Complaints of only working for the good of the corporation will be replaced by a feeling of satisfaction with how their individual and collective work has improved the world itself.

By having the foundation integrated within salesforce.com, we're not just taking—we're giving too. Our employees are happier. They're not just working at a high-pressure startup. There's a different dimension.

When the employees become wealthy people, they'll know how to make community service a part of their lives. Some of these people will go off and start their own companies, and I hope they'll replicate the model we've implemented at salesforce.com.

The 1-1-1 model—1 percent each of equity, employee time, and profits—is now the evolution of the integrated corporation. We are on the threshold of a new world. Are we creating a world in which we can all participate in value creation and at the same time provide value to those who are serving us? As corporate leaders, we can come forward and use our hard-earned leadership skills for a higher purpose—to fully integrate our globalized companies into the systems of which we are already a part.

Innovative Models

There's a saying in the philanthropic field, "If you've seen one foundation, you've seen one foundation." In other words, there's no single prescribed way for running a foundation or making grants. This is particularly true in corporate philanthropy. Some companies, as we've already seen, do their giving entirely through a foundation. Others have no foundation at all. Still others have parallel organizations—both a foundation and a corporate giving program—that split up philanthropy between them. There are obvious advantages and disadvantages to this kind of freewheeling atmosphere. The advantages include lots of room for innovation and trial and error. No one's going to pounce on you and tell you that you can't do it this way or that way. Instead, they're likely to be watching your experiment and, if it works, they might adopt your approach for their own company. The disadvantages include lack of guidance as to how a new or small company can get a philanthropic effort going, as well as possible confusion for nonprofit organizations interested in corporate partnerships.

Still, innovation is the American way, and that applies to the philanthropic side of the business just as much as the for-profit side. Indeed, corporations that take chances on their philanthropy, by introducing an unexpected design or leveraging their expertise in unusual ways or being inventive in tapping into their employees' knowledge and interests, can find themselves amply rewarded. Philanthropy, as observed in the previous chapter, is much more effective if it's integrated within the corporation, rather than treated as a silo, alone and somehow different from all the for-profit operations. Companies that pride themselves on innovative products or sales techniques should also pride themselves on innovative philanthropy. Ideally, the two go hand-in-hand. Take salesforce.com, which is coupling a new model for online delivery of software services with its integrated model for philanthropy. It even offers its software free to qualified nonprofits to help them become more innovative.

Philanthropic Structures

1. Corporate giving program, funded as a line item in community relations.

2. Marketing efforts such as event sponsorships—part of public relations budget.

3. Private foundation set up by individuals or family; can be endowed with stock from their company holdings.

4. Corporate foundation, governed by stricter giving requirements than a giving program.

5. Public charity, which serves a broader good.

6. Academy/campus program, funded from general operation budget or professional development.

7. Outsourced model, using community foundation or public fund as an intermediary.

Perhaps because innovation is its lifeblood, the technology industry has been the leader in developing cutting-edge products, such as the Internet browser and e-mail, that change the way we do business. Likewise, technology companies have often led the way in their willingness to try new approaches to philanthropy. In this chapter, we will look at two of them: IBM Corporation, which tackled one of the biggest challenges for society in "Reinventing Education," and Cisco Systems, which has done a superb job of meeting its own corporate needs while enabling philanthropic projects. But innovation is hardly confined to technology companies. We'll also take a look at two companies in far more traditional fields—office products and banking—that have been very innovative in their approaches to philanthropy. Give Something Back, the Oakland, California-based office products company, enlists philanthropy as its central mission in inducing purchases. Finally, Wells Fargo & Company, the old-line San Francisco banking company, has proven that creative philanthropy can occur even within a highly circumscribed setting, with its Community Partners program that features (seemingly) random acts of kindness.

IBM Corporation

When Louis Gerstner, a former management consultant for Mckinsey & Co., took over as CEO of IBM in 1993, there was widespread skepticism as to whether he was up to the task. But at the end of his nine-year tenure, there was nearly universal acclaim. Under Gerstner's leadership, IBM rebounded from an $8.1-billion loss in 1993 to $7.7 billion in profits in 2001, while its share price increased almost tenfold. Gerstner shifted IBM from a "products" company to a "solutions" company, focused on making things work together for its customers. Although it still supplied hardware and software, IBM also became a major consultant to technology users, utilizing its own and other companies' products to create smoothly functioning IT centers. Gerstner brought the same sensibility to IBM's philanthropy. The company had a long history of fairly traditional support of cultural and social programs, but Gerstner wanted to enable real change—bringing solutions to large, unmet needs. He seized upon education, long a favored project for technology companies, but Gerstner's thinking went way beyond delivering computers to schools or wiring them for the Internet. He actually wanted to develop tools and solutions for deep, systemic change. He called this endeavor Reinventing Education, threw IBM's formidable resources behind it ($75 million to date, plus the expertise of the company's product developers, consultants, and many others inside and outside), and tapped a former political aide/educator to run it. This was Stan Litow, who had been chancellor and chief operating officer of the New York City Board of Education, the nation's largest school system.

"I had a career working for elected officials and being chancellor in the school system," recalls Litow, who is president of the IBM Foundation and vice president of corporate community relations. Gerstner convinced him to join the corporate world by pointing out what a big, influential company such as IBM, with a commitment to corporate citizenship, could accomplish. The former CEO drew a parallel between IBM's corporate mission and its philanthropic one. Many companies provide discrete products such as computers or software, says Litow. "If you wanted to solve a complex business problem, then you needed to engage somebody with a breadth of experience," such as IBM, which provides consulting along with a range of products. "We were looking for something in the education arena that would exemplify the same attributes." When it commits to something, IBM doesn't do it in a small way. It launched Reinventing Education, or "RE," as it is known inside the company, in 1994, with $45 million that would be apportioned to schools or school districts. It has since added another $30 million to that. In the past seven years, IBM has hosted three national summits on education, attracting governors, executives, and other high-level leaders. It has also sponsored summits on Latin American education and on eLearning, the latter in conjunction with a European Commission meeting in Brussels. RE has also funded projects in 21 cities or states in the United States and nine foreign countries. The projects are all designed to implement technology—often technology developed by IBM researchers—to improve student achievement in measurable ways. (For more on actual outcomes of IBM's efforts, see Chapter 10.)

IBM links its formidable research and development (R&D) muscle to RE, with striking results that have often been lauded by Rosabeth Moss Kanter, writing in the *Harvard Business Review*. In a May-June 1999 article etitled "From Spare Change to Real Change: The Social Sector as Beta Site for Business Innovation," Kanter described how, in one school district in North Carolina, IBM created tools that allowed parents to connect to teachers digitally, letting parents view their children's schoolwork from home or a community center and compare it with the district's academic standard. IBM has also supplied technologies including data warehousing, used to give teachers and administrators access to student information; voice recognition software to teach students to read; and tracking software to enable flexible scheduling of classes.[1] According to Litow, 45 patents or patent applications for IBM have resulted from its work on RE. Not only that, "we trained a lot of our employees to work smarter and more effectively, and we developed an internal certification system" to track projects and their results.

All this let Litow effectively press his case in presentations to the IBM board and executives that investments in the RE project also paid off for the corporation. "We made the argument that we had been spending a lot of money on philanthropy that wasn't necessarily effective," he says, such as funding scholarships and after-school programs. Although these efforts help select individual students, they don't fix fundamental underlying problems with education. "We wanted to be more effective and get out of things that weren't producing return," adds Litow. The most important selling point for RE was that "we were creating intellectual capital that would help the community and eventually benefit IBM. Just like other investments in research there would be ultimate return." The idea was to create tools for learning that could also be used within IBM or elsewhere for business solutions. One product, Learning Village, was sold to a company in which IBM retained an interest. As Kanter points out in her article, the data warehousing project in Broward County, Florida, allowed the company to extend its reach "from small groups of users in retailing and related industries to very large groups of users with complicated data requirements—more than 10,000 teachers and administrators in a school system."[2]

Litow explains that "the purpose of our program is to demonstrate how IBM technology can solve problems in the public interest," thus aligning business with philanthropic interests. (For more on this approach, called strategic philanthropy, see Chapter 9.) "We look for the intractable problem that requires a solution," says Litow. "If it's something that can be developed in the research lab and be brought to scale and document specific benefit, that's the style of Reinventing Education." What IBM itself has gained from RE is internal knowledge about how to apply technology tools, some newly developed, and solutions to tackle huge, complex issues in meaningful ways. The RE project has proven that technology is not just a quick fix that boosts productivity or enables people to make prettier presentations with Microsoft PowerPoint, but an important tool for social change. As IBM and the schools with which it worked refined the approach, Big Blue was able to transfer that learning to its business customers as well.

Cisco Systems, Inc.

Cisco, the extraordinary Silicon Valley success story, has been innovative both with its foundation-based giving and with workforce development ventures more closely linked to the business side of the networking company. One of its most acclaimed programs gave laid-off workers the opportunity to work in nonprofits, an unusual step in an industry where most terminated employees are summarily escorted off the job and told not to return to the building. In fact, it was the first time any company had paid laid-off employees to work for a nonprofit. Cisco's kinder, gentler approach—although it was only available to employees who met a rigorous selection process—helped ease the pain of layoffs and provided computer skills to nonprofits. Employees were chosen based on their passion for community service (as demonstrated, for example, by previous volunteering), on whether their computer skills matched up with the needs of Cisco's nonprofit partners, and on their willingness to commit to the program for a year at much lower pay. Cisco paid these workers a third of their former salary and continued their health benefits and stock options if they worked in the nonprofit sector for a year, after which they could reapply to Cisco for available openings.

Peter Tavernise, executive director of the Cisco Foundation, was one of those employees. So were about 80 others, all of whom supplied badly needed technical expertise to nonprofits. For example, former employees hired by the Second Harvest Food Bank of Santa Clara and San Mateo Counties overhauled and upgraded the agency's technology systems, saving it $1.2 million. Other employees helped Save the Children provide satellite Internet connections to field offices in Ethiopia, Pakistan, Afghanistan, and the Philippines.[3] Cisco's creative approach to layoffs earned it goodwill in the nonprofit community, gave employees who participated a chance to continue to hone their skills and return to the company (although the majority of employees who were laid off did not get selected to participate in the program), and won it a host of admiring headlines.

Cisco's Networking Academy Program, although not formally designated as philanthropy, trains potential new computer network administrators in programs where it donates equipment and employee time across the United States and abroad. The program also has a highly regarded curriculum and certification for technology workers that is often sought out by other companies who want to offer job training in underserved communities. In Israel, for example, where salesforce.com works with Cisco, the latter company now has 28 networking academies. "We're not just teaching networking skills, but also social collaboration," says Zika Abzuk, business development manager for Cisco in Tel Aviv. She spends about 70 percent of her time on the Networking Academy Program. The first academy started in January 2002 in Nazareth, a hotbed of Arab resistance during the Palestinian intifadeh, by enrolling a group of 50 high school students—boys and girls, Jews and Arabs. Abzuk had to hold a special meeting with parents to get them to allow her to have Jews and Arabs in the same classroom. (Salesforce.com paid for the equipment and gave scholarships to the girls to attend.) The Networking Academy Program in Israel now has 300 graduates, about 55 percent of whom have landed jobs in a very tough economy. "It's the principal of giving the fishing boat rather than the fish," says Abzuk.

On the foundation side, the mission is the same: to build strong global communities, usually with technology as the enabler. Cisco has given $2 million to the Acumen Fund, which provides tools and strategies "to get something significant done in a community," says Tavernise. For instance, it has provided everything from ultra low-cost hearing aids to clean water technology to mosquito netting for poor communities in the Third World; it also helped fund a hospital in India that is an expert in cataract surgery. Closer to home, Cisco provided a five-year, $2.5-million grant to a nonprofit called CTI/Community Voice Mail in Seattle, which provides e-mail and voice-mail services for people in crisis, such as homeless families, domestic violence victims, runaway youth, migrant workers, and others to find needed resources. Cisco is also providing 30 volunteers in Seattle and three in San Jose to help

CTI go national with its platform. After Cisco's involvement, the non-profit expects to increase client enrollment by 50 percent per site and to serve 65,000 people annually by the end of the grant period. Cisco has also used technology to allow electronic filing of grant requests, greatly speeding up and smoothing out that process. "We brand what we do as 'Cisco Impact Philanthropy,'" says Tavernise.

Like IBM, Cisco applies its formidable technology expertise to important social problems. But it's more than just teaching a food bank how to use networking equipment. On the business side, Cisco fueled its explosive growth by thinking out of the box, by meshing in-house expertise with new tools developed by dozens of small companies that it has acquired over the years. On the philanthropy side, it has done the same thing. Much of what Cisco does can't really be called *philanthropy* as it's traditionally defined. Cisco has come up with new approaches that uniquely meet the company's own needs, such as workforce development and retention of talent, as well as the needs of the community, such as job opportunities and technology training.

Give Something Back

In 1991, Mike Hannigan and Sean Marx were working for a copier dealership in San Francisco when it got bought out by a bigger company. The new owner told Hannigan and Marx that they had to fire most of their staff. Instead, Hannigan and Marx left, pooling $40,000 of their own money to start an office products business. And not just any office products business. From the beginning, Give Something Back (GSB) has donated its after-tax profits to philanthropic causes in Northern California, making the company itself an instrument for social change. That now amounts to $2.5 million out of total profits of $4 million since the company was founded, says Hannigan, beginning with $1,000 in that first year. GSB donated $407,000 in 2003, compared to $406,000 in 2002. "Every year we see how much of our profits we can afford to give away without compromising our ability to grow another year," he adds. "Our model is counterintuitive because it's uncommon, not because it's nonsensical."

The two founders were inspired by the example of Paul Newman, who donates the profits from sales of his Newman's Own products, such as salad dressing and spaghetti sauce, to charity. "In the early 1990s, I was a consumer of Newman's Own," Hannigan recalls. "I bought the spaghetti sauce for the taste and price and quality. I could get my sauce and contribute to the community. It clearly worked for me as a consumer. Why wouldn't the same model work for a business consumer?" When he and Marx started GSB, "we had an entrepreneurial spirit but also a desire to do community work," says Hannigan. "We felt the Newman's Own model would work in office products and achieve our goal. At the end of the day you want to feel decent about the contribution your work is doing. We also wanted financial success. We combined our desires in the same enterprise."

GSB is not, in itself, a nonprofit organization, he emphasizes. "Our primary mission as a business is to be the best office products solution," Hannigan says. "The donating of profits in no way affects the management of the business. The marketplace determines what you have to do for success." He acknowledges that the GSB model will not work for many companies, such as publicly traded ones. "We have substituted the community—which our customers and employees help define—for the shareholders," he says. Every company donates its profits, Hannigan maintains. It's just that most do it for the shareholders. Having shareholders "competes with community interests, because the shareholders' interests are paramount," he says. In addition, GSB has no venture capital, so there's no conflict with investors who would be looking for a return on their investment rather than donating profits to the community. Hannigan also believes it would be difficult for capital-intensive industries that depend on heavy investment in R&D to adopt the GSB model. "We're dealing with products that are commodities, so our success doesn't depend on someone inventing a better mousetrap," he says. "There's no R&D. We compete on the basis of service."

However, Hannigan adds, "The fact that our profits are allocated in a different direction [than competitors] doesn't relieve us of the obligations imposed by the marketplace. We're a $28 million company in a business dominated by $10- to $12-billion competitors." He doesn't believe that his unusual disposal of after-tax profits will prevent GSB from becoming a very large company. "There are no structural reasons other than our failure to execute that would prevent us from getting to be $10- to $12-billion someday," he says. "We're the fastest-growing office products company in California." To track a competitor, he owns shares in Office Depot. As a shareholder, "I expect earnings," he says. "Being a publicly traded company results in disproportionate use of resources. Rather than complain about it, what we've chosen to do is develop an alternative model that competes for some of the existing resources and distributes them in a more equitable way."

He does concede that the GSB name and message gives the company a marketing edge. "We get all this media coverage," says Hannigan, who provided a stack of clippings from such publications as *Forbes*, the *San Francisco Chronicle*, and the *San Francisco Business Times* with articles about his company, "but with that comes accountability." When GSB approaches a customer, "we don't say we're giving something back. We say we're going to help you do your job better, spend your office products dollar better. And, by the way, we're going to donate some of our profits to the community." That has a marketing benefit, because it appeals to a customer need, Hannigan says. "There's a universal desire to give back to your community. Here's a way to do it at no cost."

GSB gives to a broad array of community organizations devoted to meeting human needs, Hannigan says. To find those, it surveys customers and employees. "We recognize the diversity of the community's needs. To get at those, you need input from a broad and diverse population. The closest we get to that is our 12,000 customers and 100 employees." Based on their input, organizations that qualify for participation are then screened by local community foundations. "Our philosophy is that the role of philanthropy is to validate community empowerment, allowing the community to take care of its problems," he says. "People who run the business should not be deciding what the needs are. There's a certain arrogance to somebody thinking that because they've done well selling widgets they can advocate for quality medical care." He believes in delegating the ultimate decisions to experts in solving community problems. "You can't be a successful businessperson and community caregiver at the same time."

Wells Fargo & Co.

When you think of conservative businesses that are set in their ways, banks are often the first that come to mind. With a century and a half of history behind it, Wells Fargo & Co., founded in 1852 in San Francisco, might seem an unlikely candidate to do innovative philanthropy. But, in fact, the banking company has found a way to enlist its hundreds of branches across the country in making local donations, and at the same time, convince branch managers to forge new relationships with the communities they serve. The bank's Community Partners program exemplifies both Wells Fargo's commitment to philanthropy—it was the largest San Francisco Bay Area giver in the 2002 survey of corporate philanthropy by the *San Francisco Business Times*—and to decentralized decision-making. CEO Dick Kovacevich says Wells views its philanthropic investments as equal in importance to any other investments the company makes, devoting 2 percent of after-tax profits to community giving. After setting that guideline, Wells leaves the selection of what nonprofits to give to in local hands. "The only way we can run a company the size of Wells is by decentralizing," notes Kovacevich. "We handle our philanthropic investments in exactly the same way. People at the local level make the decision about where to invest."

The Community Partners program is not only local in nature, it is proactive in reaching out to the community. Most philanthropy waits for nonprofits to apply for grants; Wells directs its branch managers to go out into their communities and find worthy recipients of grants, typically in the $1,000 to $1,500 range. "Our whole purpose was how we can get our bank branch managers looking at the community around them and the needs of that community," says Pamela Erwin, president of the Wells Fargo Foundation, California/Border regions. "We came up with the concept of community partners." Inaugurated in 1999, the program asks the branch managers within a Wells Fargo-served area "to step outside and identify a nonprofit and school doing really good things in their community," Erwin says. "They're supposed to go introduce themselves and hand that nonprofit a $1,000 check in totally unrestricted funding." This approach delights nonprofits, who are more accustomed to having to beg for funds. "To have a funder call us was amazing," says Britta Justesen, executive director of the Family Literacy Foundation in San Diego, the city where Wells piloted the program.

Erwin says with this upside-down model, "We have now taken a branch manager and put him or her in the role of community investigator." About 40 percent of branch managers forge lasting relationships with the nonprofits they meet this way, winding up volunteering at the organization or serving on the board. "This has been a two-pronged success story," says Erwin. In 2002, Community Partners grants totaled $636,500, benefiting 600 nonprofits. "We not only put surprise money in their coffers but made a real connection with the community," she says. "It's not about the size of the check. It's about getting out and talking with your community."

Diane De Rousseau, a Wells senior vice president and market president for San Diego, says the effort started as a pilot project there in 1998 after a survey of branch managers and senior bankers discovered that not many of them knew what Wells was doing on the philanthropy side. "We were disappointed to find out there wasn't a lot of involvement because they didn't really understand a lot about how the foundation worked," even though Wells was one of the largest corporate donors in the area. Community Partners gave branch managers "the tools to go out, do their own research, and see that personal involvement could make a difference." At the end of the first year, Wells sponsored an event to award the checks. The community partners got up to describe how the money was going to be used. "It ended up being a very emotional experience" for Wells employees, she says. "We saw how dedicated [the nonprofits] were and how far $1,000 could go." One memorable project was Habitat for Humanity's use of its $1,000 to build a house for a family in Tijuana, a Mexican border community. "It was amazing that our $1,000 could build a house," says De Rousseau. Previously, the family, like many in the area, had lived out of cardboard boxes. "These people don't have anything. Having a home was the greatest gift they could get." The Community Partners concept proved to be so popular that "we sent it [from San Diego] up to the foundation to share with the rest of the company."

Dean Thorp, regional vice president of the Wells Fargo Foundation in Southern and rural California, says community partnerships have been successful "in pushing [community giving] programs down to the team members in our banking stores [or branches]." Sometimes, he concedes, it's difficult to get busy employees to interact with the community in meaningful ways. By telling them that they had to identify someone to receive a $1,000 check, Wells got the managers to find out what nonprofits are nearby and what they need. Not only that, the model has proven itself extremely flexible in adapting to different community priorities. For example, two years ago, when California was in the grip of an energy crisis that sent utility bills soaring, service organizations were severely impacted. Thorp went out to the Palm Desert area, which depends heavily upon air conditioning, and offered checks to various nonprofits—including a childcare center, a shelter for abused women, and a senior center—to help them meet their energy needs. In the rural counties of Northern California, "we created a 'teacher of the year' program patterned after Community Partners," says Thorp. The local bank managers pulled together a committee of community members to select winners from among the nominations. Each school could have a winner, who would be awarded $500 to use for his or her classroom. After that, "we chose an overall 'teacher of the year' from among all the schools." That person got $2,000 for the classroom and another $2,000 for the school.

The Community Partners program has even created an unexpected ripple in the nonprofit community. When the nonprofits saw what some of the other organizations were doing during the San Diego award presentation, "they came to me and asked for names and contacts so they could network," says De Rousseau. So now, each year, Wells compiles the information on the community partnership gifts by community and sends it out to all the participants so they can get in touch with each other.

Inventing Philanthropy

One of the best things about philanthropy is that there are no boundaries on doing good. Community needs are so great and so underserved in most places that any well-meaning corporate philanthropic organization can probably find something to do with its money and its volunteers. Many companies write checks to local schools and nonprofits, coordinate United Way campaigns, and sponsor employee volunteer projects. All of these are beneficial. But the companies that really excel in philanthropy are the ones that bring the same imagination and verve to it that they bring to their core business. For these companies, philanthropy is not an afterthought, but as much a part of the mission as providing great service or growing profits. Serving the community doesn't have to be a tedious chore; it can be a source of delight and satisfaction for employees and executives. It can be a way to channel innovative notions from within the company to the outside world. IBM enlists its famed research lab in finding solutions for troubled schools. Cisco sends its laid-off employees to provide technical assistance for nonprofits. Wells Fargo calls on its bank managers to be Santa Claus. No one would have faulted these companies if they had been satisfied with donating only to the local United Way campaign, but they went beyond the traditional and, in doing so, enriched not only the nonprofits they serve, but also themselves.

If employees are urged to think creatively in serving their communities, that reinforces the same kind of creativity within the company. It's probably no accident that Cisco tapped a onetime laid-off worker who had participated in one of its innovative programs to come in and head its philanthropic foundation. The guy knew how to operate on a shoestring. He had to, because there's never enough of anything at a nonprofit, except for the overwhelming needs of whatever group it serves. Innovation is a tool that can be used anywhere to solve many different kinds of problems. Teach your executives and your employees to innovate in a world of severely constrained resources and large problems, and you've got a better executive or employee for your own needs. At Wells, performance reviews consider an employee's volunteerism, especially in leadership roles such as serving on a nonprofit board. "We think that's as important as their business performance," says CEO Kovacevich. At companies for whom philanthropy is a core value, performance of service within the community only enhances performance at the corporation.

Going Global

I n a company's business life, when and whether to go global is always a big decision. It can entail building or leasing new plants overseas, dealing with cultures and employees quite different from those in the United States, coping with hostile governments and activists, and expending enormous resources. But the rationale for becoming a global business is compelling too: In today's increasingly integrated, multicultural world, you lose competitive advantage by not entering every possible market. The same reasoning extends to philanthropy: In defining your community, you can't confine your service merely to the United States or North America or other cultures with which you're comfortable. "Community" expands to encompass locations where you have plants or sales outlets, or maybe where you just have customers. For example, global brands such as Coca-Cola and Levi's are known the world over. Is Coca-Cola's community where it's headquartered, where it has bottling plants, or every place where people are drinking Coke? These decisions are not easy ones, because extending philanthropy into overseas locations definitely has risks as well as rewards. "Philanthropy" does not mean the same thing in India or Albania as it does in the United States; in Japan, there is no word at all for *philanthropy*. When companies extend a helping hand in these places, they must be even more careful about communicating expectations up front—to governments, nonprofits, and the people they're trying to help. Otherwise, well-meaning intentions, sadly, could backfire, leading to misunderstanding and tension.

Still, the rewards of doing global philanthropy more than justify the hassle. First of all, the needs of many developing countries are so overwhelming that companies doing business there must consider community service on a purely humanitarian basis. It's difficult for a business to prosper when the community around it is suffering, for a company needs educated, willing, healthy workers. To be sure, providing jobs can improve a community's level of prosperity, but is that enough? There remain such issues as access to education and healthcare, exercise of human rights, and being able to feed oneself and one's family.

The first model of philanthropy was family-owned companies that were very identified with the communities where they built their businesses and felt an obligation to give back. But oftentimes that obligation did not extend very far beyond the headquarters city. With today's multinational corporations—when even small companies such as salesforce.com go global very early in their existence—and our increasing interdependence as a planet, community service can no longer be parochial. Companies must look at the whole world as their potential community, and then thoughtfully select areas where their philanthropy is most needed and can have the greatest impact, based on their mission and program focus areas.

The companies profiled in this chapter have done just that. Levi Strauss & Co., which operates owned or leased plants in about 60 countries, has not been afraid to teach workers about their rights, even when they may voice complaints about Levi itself. Starbucks Coffee Company works with farmers to set up buffers around biodiversity preserves in coffee-growing regions. LensCrafters, all of whose retail optical stores are located in North America, nonetheless saw such an opportunity for service in the Third World that it started missions there to deliver glasses. Those missions have now reached 1 million people in about 25 countries (see Chapter 2 for how LensCrafters defined that mission). Finally, salesforce.com, a small company with only a few hundred employees, has made a difference in helping young Arabs and Jews in the Middle East find some common ground.

6 Principles of Global Philanthropy

1. Assure that the global mission fits with the company's business and philanthropic strategy.

2. Study the cultural, societal, and business structures of the countries involved. Tailor philanthropy to accommodate those.

3. Actively involve local employees by seeking their input and engaging them in projects.

4. Partner with expert organizations that have a presence in and understanding of the country.

5. Provide for cross-cultural interaction among executives, local leaders, and employees.

6. Work with local government organizations so they can champion your cause and smooth your way.

Levi Strauss & Co.

As an apparel manufacturer, Levi can't dodge the burning issue of sweatshops and cheap labor in Third World countries. "You have to understand that sweatshops is the issue in our field," says Theresa Fay-Bustillos, executive director of the Levi Strauss Foundation. Adds Levi CEO Phil Marineau, "Apparel companies chase low-cost labor and low tariffs. We produce in 60 countries around the world. If we don't do this, we don't survive or remain competitive in the marketplace." At the same time, says Marineau, with both its owned plants and those under contract, "morally, we have the same responsibility. We believe we should provide a safety net of services, and that's what we're trying to do in the communities where we're located." As described in Chapter 5, even when Levi closes down a plant, it doesn't pull out of the community. "Our philosophy has been to go back in with foundation money and provide economic education and create substitute employment for the jobs being lost," says Marineau.

Fay-Bustillos, a former civil rights attorney, says Levi has chosen to focus on educating workers at its contractors' plants about their rights. The company itself developed a code of ethics to monitor these factories in 1991. "The lens we have chosen to use at the foundation is legal rights and social protections," she says. Many of Levi's overseas workers are women holding their first jobs and away from home for the first time. "They don't know how to manage their money. They may also do unwise things like engaging in unsafe sexual practices," due to loneliness and ignorance about protection. Levi uses foundation grants to partner with nonprofits that help these workers obtain access to basic healthcare, learn how to prevent HIV/AIDS and other sexually transmitted diseases, and get financial literacy training. In addition, says Fay-Bustillos, "if you look at countries in the developing world, many have great labor laws on the books, but they're not enforced." Not only does Levi set up workshops to teach workers about their rights, it also funds nonprofits that employ lawyers to help enforce the laws. "Workers need to be able to go somewhere and do something about these types of problems," she says. "When you're going to empower people to have rights, you have to give them a way to exercise those rights." Even when they come back with complaints about Levi factories, "that's what we want," says Fay-Bustillos. "We want to hear if there's an issue so we can go in and try to address it."

In one example of its overseas work, Levi has partnered with the Asia Foundation to fund training for migrant workers who are moving into the Pearl River Delta, an area in coastal China where many factories are located. A law on the books in China requires factories to give health checkups to workers, but few were doing it, Fay-Bustillos reports. "We gave incentive grants to factories to bring doctors into the plants to do the checkups." Another grant helps train union representatives, who, in Chinese plants, are selected by management, on worker rights issues. Those union representatives, in turn, "go into the factories and train workers." But even that wasn't sufficient for Levi. "We still weren't creating enough change," she says. The company discovered that, although China has a legal aid system, it didn't benefit migrant workers, because they were not considered residents of the area where they worked, but rather of the city where they were born. "So we gave a grant to the Women's Bureau, who started a legal aid bureau focused on migrant workers," says Fay-Bustillos. Now, she adds with a smile, "that program has been so successful that the regular bureau wants to take on some of these cases." Another small grant helped start a newspaper for workers written by workers. "It has a column with questions and answers about workers' rights," she says. "We also started a hotline for workers to call in with questions."

Outside the factory, Levi wanted to help fulfill the migrant workers' social needs. "A lot of these workers are very lonely and far from home," lacking a social network, says Fay-Bustillos. Partnering again with the Asia Foundation, Levi provided a grant that allowed workers to create an entertainment troupe. When she traveled recently to China, Fay-Bustillos attended one of the performances on a Sunday evening. "You go there and you see all these workers walking to the amphitheater," she recalls. Some of the workers themselves put on the show. The highlight of the evening came when one worker performed a long, sad song (translated for the American visitors). "I looked around me and all the audience was crying," says Fay-Bustillos. Then she got the translation. "It was a song about the different regions of China." As the song finished, "the sobbing workers (lonely for family and friends back home) jumped up in applause."

Levi goes where it has a business presence, which equals a sales office or a factory it owns or with which it contracts. "This is too substantial to manage from San Francisco," says Fay-Bustillos. "I don't see how you can do worldwide grantmaking without a worldwide staff." She has grantmakers in Miami, for Latin America and Canada; in Brussels, for Europe and Africa; and in Singapore, for Asia. Before it decides where to make grants overseas, Levi does considerable research and planning. "We look at the business, economic, and social issues. We also look at our assets," Fay-Bustillos says. In many locations, Levi employees have formed Community Involvement Teams (CITs) to volunteer with and donate funds to community agencies. So she and her foundation management consider whether to rely solely upon CITs or whether a grantmaking strategy would be effective and make a difference. "We do the analysis and plot the region; then we figure out a three-year grant-making plan," she says. Some places will just have CITs; others might just get grants because employee volunteerism is weak. "You have to leverage your money and resources to make a difference," Fay-Bustillos says. "Otherwise you're spread way too thin, giving $20,000 to the starving in India."

In many areas of the world, philanthropy is not a strong tradition the way it is in the United States. Consequently, Levi must develop its own tradition through the company. "Our employees feel like they're part of a global company, so they recognize that they're a part of this tradition of giving," says Fay-Bustillos. "They're willing to break with some of their own traditions to be part of working here. We create a culture of volunteering." Two years ago she addressed a meeting in Malaysia attended by the top 100 Levi managers from Asia. "We always put community affairs on the agenda at these meetings," she says, as part of nurturing a culture of service. When she spoke, Fay-Bustillos asked everyone in the audience who had done volunteer work in the community during the last year to stand. About 80 percent stood up. Then she asked, of those standing, how many gave money. About three-fourths of the group remained standing. "You can break through stereotypes," Fay-Bustillos says. "After I spoke, I had lines of people waiting to talk to me about getting involved in community affairs." CEO Marineau reports a similar experience when he went to Manila to celebrate Levi's 30th anniversary in the Philippines. He asked the employees to show him what they were proud of. "The first thing they did was take us to the community development center." Each employee had contributed $10 to open the center, which helped women to start their own small businesses. The center is a prime example of how to leverage resources. "Sometimes a small amount of funding can make a huge difference," Marineau says.

Starbucks Coffee Company

Like Levi, Seattle-based Starbucks often runs into a buzz saw of criticism over issues of globalization and what to pay suppliers in poor countries. As of mid-2003, Starbucks had 3,645 coffeehouses in North America and 1,451 either company-operated or licensed in other locations. The company has both a foundation, started in 1997, and a corporate giving program, and the two have distinctly separate functions. Lauren Moore, who directs corporate giving as well as the foundation, says the foundation does what is considered "pure philanthropy," while the giving program focuses on efforts where marketing is a component. "We don't want to cross the line between pure philanthropy and a PR benefit," she says. Consequently, the foundation, which was jump-started with royalties from a book by CEO Howard Schultz called *Pour Your Heart Into It: How Starbucks Built a Company One Cup at a Time*, devotes itself to childhood and youth literacy programs in North America. The corporate giving program has a global reach, focusing on the environment and coffee-growing regions where Starbucks has suppliers. According to Moore, "The corporate giving budget gives us more flexibility" to look at projects that combine a marketing/public relations benefit for the corporation with charitable donation.

The primary example is Starbucks' work supporting Conservation International (CI), which is "trying to preserve big swathes of the planet for wildlife diversity," says Moore. Starbucks and Conservation International have a pilot project involving the El Triunfo Biosphere Reserve in Chiapas, Mexico. The idea is to surround the biodiversity preserve with coffee farms. "We're working to support the coffee farmers because it provides a buffer," she says. "We get the business benefit because what the farmers grow is shade-grown, organically grown coffee," which is both environmentally correct and a selling point for customers. At the same time, Starbucks provides grants to CI to do its preservation work. On a global basis, "Much of our [philanthropic] investment has to do with improving our own environmental footprint and operating in an environmentally appropriate way," Moore says.

The work with CI began in 1998, when the nonprofit approached Starbucks. "The purpose from the beginning has been to make coffee production a force for biodiversity conservation," says Glenn Prickett, senior vice president of CI. The Washington, D.C.-based nonprofit had observed that areas where coffee grows are also areas of high biodiversity. "A lot of rain forests and cloud forests were being cleared for coffee production," says Prickett. But traditional techniques of growing coffee in the shade of these forests don't require clearing of the land. "So our goal was to encourage growers to use traditional growing that doesn't have as much [environmental] impact." Not only that, the coffee-growing areas can stabilize a biodiversity tract by acting as a buffer because "it has better habitat value than other agricultural uses," Prickett says. CI wanted a partner who would buy coffee from these traditional growers, and it found that in Starbucks, plus a generous philanthropic donor. The coffee retailer provided an initial grant of $150,000 and, as of early 2003, had contributed about $2.5 million to CI's efforts. CI largely uses the money to provide technical assistance to farmers, both on business practices such as negotiating prices and on sustainable agriculture. Beyond the grants, Starbucks also commits to provide a market for the shade-grown coffee, paying premium prices. "If you're a poor campesino living in Mexico you can get a much better price selling to Starbucks than to local coffee traders," says Prickett. "That gives farmers incentive to use good conservation practices." In 2002, more than 1,000 farmers were participating in the program, with 7,400 acres under cultivation. The farmers received an 87 percent premium over local prices for their shade-grown coffee, according to Starbucks. CI and Starbucks have now begun similar projects in Colombia and Peru; future plans include expansion to Panama and Costa Rica.

Because of Starbucks's prominent position as a global U.S. multinational with a worldwide retail presence, organizations such as CI, not to mention protesters, "will target Starbucks," Moore notes. "We provide a platform for them to voice their opinions, because they know we will listen. We do make an effort to engage people, but we also try to carefully screen what's appropriate." Take its 11-year alliance with CARE, (Cooperative for Assistance and Relief Everywhere, Inc.), an international organization dedicated to fighting global poverty in more than 60 countries. In 1989, the Northwest regional director for CARE was standing in line at a local Starbucks when he picked up a brochure that showed the countries where the company bought coffee. Almost all of them overlapped with CARE locations. Starbucks subsequently chose CARE as a conduit for giving back to coffee-origin countries with community development and emergency relief grants. Starbucks has contributed or raised more than $2 million for CARE programs, making it one of the agency's largest North American corporate donors. "We always want to position ourselves with a national organization that is an expert," Moore says.

LensCrafters, Inc.

All of the locations of the optical retail firm LensCrafters are in North America. It really has no global presence. Why, then, has it gone on missions to 25 different countries in the last dozen years? "We go international not because we have markets there, but because the particular product we wanted to share had to be taken outside the country," says Susan Knobler, vice president of the LensCrafters Foundation, which oversees its Gift of Sight program (see Chapters 2 and 3). LensCrafters, in partnership with local Lions Clubs International, takes recycled, refurbished glasses to poor countries where people could not otherwise afford vision care. (The United States has laws prohibiting reuse of glasses.) On each mission to a foreign country, about 25 LensCrafters employees participate, matching the glasses, performing vision tests, and doing the fittings. So the second motivation for LensCrafters's global approach is to give employees an unmatched experience spending two weeks overseas, helping people and learning about another culture. "We had an option to ship the glasses to other groups to do this," says Knobler, "but we decided, who better than we has the talent and resources and energetic young people?" The opportunity to participate in one of the missions is highly sought by employees, who must be selected based on their skills and their volunteerism. "What an amazing experience to give to an employee," says Knobler. She compares it to the reality-TV show *Survivor*, except "it's better because you're helping people, not voting someone off the island."

In 1991 LensCrafters did its first mission to Costa Rica. By mid-2003 it had completed 56 missions and helped 1 million people internationally. Knobler explains that LensCrafters depends on the Lions Clubs to handle the international contacts, such as writing a letter to the local ministry of health and obtaining the necessary permits. In addition, wherever LensCrafters holds its clinic, "we need to have about 50 people a day volunteering as translators and providing other help," she says. "We see 3,000 people a day." The only time LensCrafters had to close down a mission before its scheduled end was in 1995, when it went to Albania without support from a local Lions Clubs. The former Communist nation just wasn't able to follow the rules. "All of the these Communist-affiliated big shots wanted us to help them first and let them go to the front of the line," recalls Knobler, who went on that mission herself. When LensCrafters refused, the company wound up leaving in two days. For the present, though, LensCrafters is avoiding going to Muslim nations because of the possible threat to employees' safety. "We have never had any incident on an international trip and we want to keep it that way," says Knobler. However, she won't hesitate to return to Muslim countries when she believes the time is right. In the past, LensCrafters has gone to Morocco, Tunisia, and the Philippines, all of which have high concentrations of Muslims. "Once we have a good relationship, we will go back to that country," she says.

Knobler says the missions provide extraordinary diversity training and bonding opportunities for employees, who are selected from all over North America. At the same time, "over the years we've learned that we have to be quite strict with our team members," she adds. "They're still on company payroll and time, so we have implemented a code of conduct." Although LensCrafters wants employees to have fun and builds in a day of rest and relaxation at the end of each mission, "it's not about seeing the country, it's about helping these people," says Knobler. To that end, employees do not get to select where they want to go; that's decided by LensCrafters.

Mark Durkan, a senior operations manager for the LensCrafters Foundation, has led 28 overseas missions, the most recent to Peru in July 2003. "It's definitely taken my life in a different direction," he says. "You experience the culture in a way that a tourist never does." Although LensCrafters pays for employee accommodations at a decent hotel, "we're often invited into the homes of the people for a meal. You interact with them on their level." He also assigns an employee on each mission to learn more about the culture and line up a speaker or two to present to the entire group. In 1998, he remembers going to Bangladesh, where the LensCrafters contingent stayed at a new hotel in Dhakka, the capital. Durkan remembers looking outside from his 17th-floor room to the beautiful pool, while just beyond the wall surrounding the pool was a swamp jammed with hovels. "It's so overcrowded and polluted," he says. "You can't believe the contrast between the hotel and what's outside."

In leading all these missions, he has learned not to count on the precise time-tables to which Americans are accustomed. In Bangladesh, "the clinic that was supposed to be four hours away was more like 12 hours away," thanks to waiting for ferries and other means of transportation. The clinic was a hospital complex in the local chief's home village. "This was such a unique service we brought that the lines on both sides (men and women were in separate queues) were over a quarter mile long," Durkan recalls. "We can do up to 4,000 people a day," he adds, but when the group was done in Bangladesh, it had helped so many, "we didn't even have any more rubbing alcohol to wipe down our machines." The record mission, though, was December 2002 to Thailand, when 33,000 people got vision tests and eyeglasses in two weeks.

Durkan agrees with Knobler that the experience touches employees in ways that almost nothing else could. It also offers new perspective on how we live in the United States versus other parts of the world. "Typically, when I come back from a mission, I get into this whole kick about simplifying my life," Durkan says. "I start getting rid of extra stuff. And getting stuck in traffic isn't as big a deal—I have a car with air conditioning and a stereo." More seriously, he says, the missions "give people from different parts of the company and different social backgrounds a chance to interact." For example, an executive always accompanies the missions, and for many employees, it's their first chance to interact with someone who determines the direction of the company. "It levels the playing field," he says. "When you have a company conference people are always mindful of what their rank is. When you're on the mission, you forget about all that."

Salesforce.com

Salesforce.com, even though it's still a small company with about 600 employees, has found several means of doing philanthropy on a worldwide basis. The first is that once an overseas sales office reaches "critical mass," around 30 to 40 people, Suzanne DiBianca, the executive director of the salesforce.com Foundation, hires a permanent foundation person at the location to coordinate philanthropic and volunteer activities. The second is to aid its individual executives in establishing what are called donor-advised funds through the foundation, permitting the executive to pursue a passionate interest in areas such as Israel, India, and Nepal. While salesforce.com has little or no presence in those countries, it does have executives with ties to the cultures who make donations of their own funds. The foundation gives the executives support on directing and managing the funds and does small matches where possible. The third is similar: Salesforce.com allows employees who have an interest in a particular country to inaugurate a project there and provides some matching support in funds or donated equipment. For example, one employee had a tremendous dedication to doing something in Africa; he raised money, acquired donated computers, and got a match from the salesforce.com Foundation to travel to Africa and wire up computers for a local school. He used his six days of paid service to cover the trip.

Salesforce.com also partners with other companies, notably Cisco Systems, to do philanthropy in geographically remote areas. The previous chapter described Cisco's Networking Academy Program. In Israel, the salesforce.com Foundation has donated equipment and funding to networking academies where young Jews and Arabs study together. Salesforce.com and Cisco have also teamed up on a project to provide technology training to women in ultra Orthodox communities. Within those communities, "the men study all day and the women must provide for their families," says Zika Abzuk, business development manager for Cisco in Tel Aviv and coordinator of its networking academies. "We thought they could do this by mastering a needed technological profession." Salesforce.com donated the equipment to set up the class, as it did for a similar endeavor among high school dropouts, many of them Russian immigrants, in a tough neighborhood in Tel Aviv. "They were teaching these kids hairdressing and carpentry," says Abzuk. Cisco offered them networking training, and now four of the students are working at the company's research lab there.

Even when salesforce.com doesn't have an office in a country, if its employees have an interest, so does the company. After the war in Afghanistan, "our employees were very interested in helping that country to rebuild," recalls DiBianca. United States-based employees got the company to donate 25 older computers, which they upgraded by installing the latest software, and gave the refurbished computers to the United Nations for use in a women's economic development center. Another salesforce.com employee with ties to Romania wanted to open a computer center there. "He donated his own money, and we did a small match and were able to put in a technology center in Romania," says DiBianca. "If employees feel strongly about something and are willing to give their time, the foundation will do what it can," she says. As a general rule, DiBianca prefers to have at least two employees involved in a project, "so if one leaves, we still have a link left in the other."

By the end of 2003, salesforce.com had foundation coordinators in London, Ireland, and Tokyo. DiBianca says the impetus for this globalization is "our whole model for integration." She adds, "If you're trying to build a similar culture [of philanthropy] everywhere in the world, you need to drive it early. We think 30 people is the right critical mass to get started." There are enough people in the office for some to begin participating in volunteer projects. "Anywhere we have a big presence, we believe we should be giving back," says DiBianca. The approach is similar to that used in the United States, although tailored for cultural differences. In many countries there is little tradition of formal giving the way there is in the United States. Instead, employees there are going to do philanthropy revolving around helping the employed. "Unemployment has become a big issue in Japan," notes DiBianca. "People can understand the importance of companies giving help to retrain older workers." She says that overcoming cultural barriers depends on enlisting local employees in the philanthropic effort. "You just do what the people there are passionate about," she says. "It has to be driven by employees. We give them room to be creative."

It's a Small World

Companies such as Levi and Starbucks know that they're part of a worldwide community because they get criticized for their actions in seemingly remote parts of the globe. To their credit, both companies recognized their responsibility to this worldwide community and took action to respond to its needs. The powerful element in what both companies are doing is that they chose philanthropic efforts with a close link to the company's interests so that giving could be channeled effectively and impactfully. In Levi's case, that meant giving grants for educating factory workers about their rights and even for providing wholesome entertainment. In Starbucks's model, which clearly mixes business with philanthropic goals, the company provides coffee farmers with the needed expertise to implement environmentally friendly agriculture, and then is willing to pay a premium for their product, thus giving them an incentive to stick with the program.

Smaller companies, such as LensCrafters and salesforce.com, that don't have significant overseas contingents can also get involved. LensCrafters's far-reaching missions to provide glasses to people in third-world countries provide tremendous benefits, not just to the people helped, but to its employees doing the helping. Many companies invest large sums in "bonding programs" that compel executives and employees to travel to unusual locations and engage in nerve-jangling activities such as rappelling up a cliff. LensCrafters found a way to combine doing good and giving employees memorable life experiences at the same time. Salesforce.com enables its employees to exercise their creativity and pursue their passion for helping. By having foundation expertise in overseas offices, the company makes sure that its culture of philanthropy is truly integrated and not just a U.S. phenomenon. All of these companies' efforts demonstrate that, while the notion of formalized philanthropy may not be universal, the willingness to help one's fellow human beings is. And companies can reap goodwill for themselves and their employees by tapping into that powerful sentiment.

Strategic Philanthropy
(or Not)

One of the burning debates for corporate philanthropy has always been how much to exploit the public relations benefit of doing good. Some companies prefer to do what they call "pure philanthropy," which they consider philanthropy that doesn't have a marketing component built in. Others go to the other extreme with cause-related marketing—backing high-profile, popular events such as the Olympics. And there are gradations in between. Corporate giving comes in as many forms as the Jewish philosopher Maimonides' eight levels of charity, and then some. For Maimonides, the highest form of charity was helping someone to help themselves, which is certainly the aim of the majority of corporate philanthropy. The phrase "we want to teach someone to fish rather than give them fish" is heard over and over in interviews with corporate philanthropists. But ultimately—let's be honest—corporations do philanthropy because it has benefits for them, whether in making the CEO feel good or in retaining employees and teaching them new skills or in garnering public admiration. So how far should corporations go in combining philanthropy with their own business goals? The question elicits all kinds of controversy, among both the corporate community and the nonprofit one.

Maimonides' Eight Levels of Charity

8. The greatest level is to strengthen another person by giving him a present or loan, or making a partnership with him, or finding him a job so that he no longer needs to beg from people.

7. Below this is the one who gives to the poor, but does not know to whom he gives, nor does the recipient know his benefactor.

6. Below this is one who knows to whom he gives, but the recipient does not know his benefactor.

5. Below this is one who does not know to whom he gives, but the poor person does know his benefactor.

4. Below this is one who gives to the poor person before being asked.

3. Below this is one who gives to the poor person after being asked.

2. Below this is one who gives to the poor person gladly and with a smile.

1. Below this is one who gives to the poor person unwillingly.

(Excerpted from Maimonides, *Mishneh Torah*, Laws of Presents to the Poor, as translated by Jonathan J. Baker.)

Two gurus who claim to have the answer are Michael Porter, a well-known business strategist and author of *Competitive Advantage*, and Mark Kramer, a former nonprofit fund-raiser turned consultant. They also run the Foundation Strategy Group in Boston, which advises foundations on how to leverage their donations to have more impact. In December 2002, Kramer and Porter wrote an influential and provocative article in the *Harvard Business Review* titled "The Competitive Advantage of Corporate Philanthropy." In that article, they state flatly that corporate philanthropy should be designed to give corporations a leg up on competitors. "Philanthropy can often be the most cost-effective way—and sometimes the only way—to improve competitive context. It enables companies to leverage not only their own resources, but also the existing efforts and infrastructure of nonprofits and other institutions," they write.[1] For example, the authors approvingly describe Cisco's networking academies, which train young people to be network administrators, giving them needed job skills while, at the same time, enhancing Cisco's ability to grow by providing essential IT support for users of its technology. They also laud the pharmaceutical manufacturer Pfizer for donating drugs to prevent trachoma, a leading cause of blindness, in developing countries. At the same time, Pfizer worked with a nonprofit to create the infrastructure to distribute its drugs within potential new markets, enhancing its long-term business prospects.

Although Kramer and Porter debunk what is widely referred to as "strategic philanthropy," by saying that most of it is neither strategic nor philanthropic, they nonetheless are advocates. "True strategic giving...addresses important social and economic goals simultaneously, targeting areas of competitive context where the company and society both benefit because the firm brings unique assets and expertise."[2] Many in corporate and nonprofit philanthropy view Kramer and Porter's ideas warily, to say the least, but the two consultants have turned the spotlight upon a critical issue that deserves discussion—balancing business and philanthropic goals. In this chapter, we explore several corporations that have embraced so-called strategic philanthropy—including Hewlett-Packard, Microsoft, and Coca-Cola—and contrast them with two that have not—General Motors and Adobe Systems.

Hewlett-Packard Company

Back in 1939, not long after Bill Hewlett and David Packard founded their namesake company in the famous garage that's now considered the birthplace of Silicon Valley, they donated $5 to the forerunner of United Way. "We have a long history at HP of encouraging our people, as individuals, to participate in projects and organizations aimed at benefiting their local communities or the broader society," wrote David Packard in *The HP Way*. "We stress to our people that each of these communities [where HP operates] must be better for our presence…it means contributing talent, energy, time, and financial support to community projects."[3] In 2002, HP donated $62.2 million, including cash and product gifts, to philanthropic efforts, making it the second largest giver among computing companies in the United States (behind only IBM). That total went primarily to schools and underserved communities, as HP concentrated the giving to meet its recently defined focus on education and community and economic development around the world.

Bess McDowell Stephens, HP's vice president of philanthropy and education, recalls that, after Carly Fiorina took over as CEO of HP in mid-1999, the company decided "to step back and take a careful look at the focus we had in corporate giving." Previously, the approach had been reactive, responding to requests. "We had a lot of different buckets," including the arts, culture, environment, and charitable giving, says Stephens. "We were doing 'spray and pray.'" The new approach "is to determine the key areas of focus and review that periodically." Hewlett-Packard came up with two primary areas of emphasis: education, which had been a longstanding interest, and what it calls "e-inclusion," or making technology accessible to underserved areas and groups (see next chapter for more on that). "There are clear reasons why we believe education is one of the most fundamental areas," she says. "You can make the greatest impact in a variety of different ways, and it's important to the community and our company." The new executive team at HP had a good deal of input into the philanthropic focuses. "We determined we could have a much greater impact and leverage our results by being more proactive," Stephens says. "That's the reason for identifying these two areas. They allow us to go deeper and have substantially more impact."

"When we do philanthropy, it's not just projects hanging out there funded through third parties," adds Debra Dunn, senior vice president of corporate affairs and a 20-year veteran of HP. "Writing a check is not much skin in the game. Increasingly, we think challenges in the world are big ones, particularly education and e-inclusion. For us, as a company, we want to bring more of HP's capabilities to solving that problem rather than just writing a check." Fiorina is a staunch proponent of the new approach, Dunn says. "Carly was very clear that we needed to continue the strong tradition of giving back. She elevated the level of strategic thinking."

Of course, defining these focus areas for HP's corporate giving meant that some nonprofits to which it had traditionally donated got cut off. Stephens says HP worked closely with those to help ease the transition. "Nonprofits that apply for grants have a good understanding that things change. We've explained the changes that were going on in the company to them," she says. "We've not had a lot of the negative reaction to what we're doing. They want to understand how they can participate in the new strategy." For those that don't fit, HP still allocates a certain amount for local giving and for unexpected events such as disasters, and it does employee matching, "so there are other venues for which people can apply," Stephens notes. When HP merged with Compaq in 2002, it had some similar decisions to make about what philanthropy from that company to keep and what to eliminate. The new focus areas helped in making the decision. "We'd already narrowed our focus. We had the opportunity to review the same issues (of strategy) as we prepared for the merger," says Stephens. "We'd had good practice." Compaq had a number of partnerships with large national organizations, some of which HP decided to retain, including TechCorp and Boys & Girls Clubs. With others, "we had to make the call that this particular investment is not aligned with what we're doing," says Stephens. "We'd tell the latter organizations that we'd continue to fund them until 2003 to give them time to make a transition."

Despite the hard decisions to eliminate or reduce funding in some places, "it has been very exciting and exhilarating to map out this new proactive approach," she says. In fact, it has even invigorated HP's nonprofit relationships (for more on those, see the next chapter). "These organizations that come to us have a vision of their own self-sufficiency, which is very compatible with how we've positioned ourselves," says Stephens. "Everyone aspires to have the capability and the skills to be gainfully engaged in the economic dynamic of whatever region they live in. If we can move that forward on their behalf, that's a far better strategy than just reacting to arbitrary proposals that come in. We're reinventing the company, and we have a new model of philanthropy that's congruent with that."

Microsoft Corporation

Microsoft, the world's largest software company, has a couple of unique problems when it comes to philanthropy. The first is the fact that its cofounder, former CEO, and chairman, Bill Gates, is one of the world's foremost philanthropists in his own right with the $24-billion Bill and Melinda Gates Foundation, which tends to overshadow whatever Microsoft is doing on its own. The second is the company's long battle with the U.S. Department of Justice over its alleged monopolistic practices, making the Microsoft name rather notorious. Acknowledges Pamela Passman, director of global corporate affairs, "We probably were a bit quiet about what we were doing (philanthropically) when there were so many other issues 'monopolizing' the newspapers." Perhaps to avoid any confusion with the Gates Foundation, Microsoft has no corporate foundation, but instead has a corporate giving program within the company. "We've been able to do what we wanted and to grow the contributions without a foundation," says Passman. Creating a foundation "is something that we think about, talk about, but have had no specific reason to do up to this point."

In fiscal 2002, Microsoft donated $40 million in cash and another $207 million in in-kind contributions of its software to nonprofits. Passman says that, in the past, Microsoft had a very "popgun" approach to philanthropy, but in the last couple of years, with the involvement of Gates and CEO Steve Ballmer, has moved to focus in on four specific areas, or "pillars." Those areas are: expanding opportunities through technology access, strengthening nonprofits through technology, developing a diverse technology workforce, and building community through corporate funding and matching employees' individual giving. Now the company is further refining that focus by introducing a new program called Unlimited Potential (UP). "For people to have really meaningful access to economic and societal opportunities, they need to have the IT skills," says Passman. UP, which made its first round of grants in 2003 in outlays worth $4 million, aims to provide technology skills through community learning centers. The grants covered the costs of establishing curriculum, creating training materials, and hiring staff. The next step will be development of a support network where the learning centers can share best practices online and offline. Finally, Microsoft will offer a venture award fund recognizing programs or applications that could have a wider societal impact.

"As we set out on a path to focus our philanthropy, we spent time surveying governments, international organizations, and NGOs to hear what should Microsoft should be doing," says Passman. "Through this process, we heard very loud and clear: They want us engaged in what we know best," which, of course, is delivering technology. Consequently, Microsoft is a proponent of the Porter/Kramer philosophy on corporate philanthropy. "It's quite rational to align what you do best with how you contribute," says Passman. "We want to be engaged, we want to contribute, and we can do a lot more of that with the resources we work with every day." One example is Microsoft's HEART program, which stands for Humanitarian Empower and Relief through Technology. A couple of applications have resulted. One is a food and commodity tracking system that, similar to what FedEx does with its packages, allows nonprofits to find out where disaster relief supplies are and reroute them, if necessary. Another application is a Pocket PC tool to do health and vulnerability assessments in remote areas such as Africa. A third revolves around Microsoft's alliances with Boys & Girls Clubs; it provides technology to integrate the 2,600 clubs nationally and at U.S. military bases abroad. Microsoft doesn't eschew any relationship with the Gates Foundation. It is partnering with the private foundation in donating software aimed at expanding public access to computing and the Internet at public libraries. The five-year goal for the Gates Foundation is to reach 11,000 libraries serving low-income communities in the United States and Canada.

Although much of its philanthropy involves utilizing technology effectively, Microsoft does considerable non-technology giving to communities in which it has offices, especially the Puget Sound area of Washington, where it's headquartered. Most of this occurs through employee matching. "We are a significant employer, so we have a program to contribute to different organizations that don't necessarily fit our four pillars," Passman says. In the United States, Microsoft employees contribute more than $20 million annually, and the company matches that up to $12,000 a year per employee. "Our employees contribute to all types of nonprofits, including the arts, environment, health, and human services," she says. "In communities where we have a significant presence, there are responsibilities that go with that which have nothing to do with technology."

Coca-Cola Company

Like Microsoft, Levi, and Starbucks, Coca-Cola is another multinational that has an extraordinarily well-known brand name closely linked with the United States, entailing both negatives and positives for the company. Its philanthropy, naturally, seeks to exploit the positives and downplay the negatives with a new strategic focus on the environment, which Coca-Cola affects directly with its manufacturing processes and indirectly with the waste generated by millions of cans and bottles. The stated intent is to "create value in all our relationships within the environmental community through demonstrating leadership in each critical environmental impact area: water, energy, resource, and solid waste management, both in our operations and in the community and marketplace." This is accomplished through Coca-Cola's five regional business units, and the intent evolved after the company decentralized in 2000, pushing down resources and management to 25 operating divisions within the five units. "As part of that, we were handed partnerships with nonprofits and told to work with them," recalls Ben Jordan, environmental manager at Coca-Cola North America in Atlanta. Some of the support came from the corporate foundation budget, but some of it was expected to be provided locally.

When he took a look at the partnerships, it was a hodge-podge with about two dozen different organizations. "A lot of those partnerships were old, where some [Coca-Cola] vice president knew somebody who was the executive director," says Jordan. "Our whole goal was to get beyond that and be more strategic. We didn't necessarily want to delete people, but we wanted to understand why we were partnering and make it meaningful." With that goal in mind, he organized a daylong meeting in Atlanta in April 2001, with representatives of all the partnering nonprofits, which include such organizations as Keep America Beautiful, the Nature Conservancy, and the Georgia Recycling Coalition. "The partners left knowing more about the Coca-Cola Company and what we were trying to do. And we understood more of what they were trying to do," says Jordan. This was followed by a second meeting in April 2002 that got down to specifics, with breakout sessions on water, solid waste and resource management, and energy and global climate change. With another meeting planned in mid-2003, Jordan says he's making progress toward his goal: "We've got to be partnering in a more strategic way with groups that understand what we're doing." Coca-Cola wants to reduce its own impact on the environment and partner with groups that can help the company deliver that message. "Our partners can tell us what outside people expect from us and they can also be our voices out in the external community, helping us communicate what we're trying to do," he says.

Jordan has made a first pass at sorting through some of the partnerships. "We've cut off a couple of groups just not fitting with the mission," he says. For example, the company had a partnership with Wildlife Habitat Council, which helps corporations put conservation programs in place on their corporate lands. The council "does great work," Jordan says, but because Coca-Cola doesn't really have any large land holdings, "they're not a good fit for us." Even though Coca-Cola had been writing membership checks for five years, "we'd never done a project." With other organizations, such as the Nature Conservancy, Coca-Cola worked to find projects that fit with its goals. Jordan has an annual budget of around $800,000, and he makes contributions ranging from $1,000 to $200,000 a year. Partners are designated as *strategic, sustaining*, and *supporting*. Generally, strategic partners, such as Keep America Beautiful, the Nature Conservancy, and the National Park Foundation, get the most resources; sustaining partners get the next highest amount of resources and supporting partners, the least. Jordan says that, as he makes donations, "we are pushing groups to communicate to us what they did with the money, what projects they funded." He wants to make sure that nobody is measuring success solely on the basis of dollars raised. He also encourages nonprofits to work with each other to minimize the competition for funding. "We need to have all our water groups get along," he says.

Another change that Coca-Cola has made is to be more approachable to nonprofits that have complaints about its environmental policies. "If they've got a gripe, we should listen to that and evaluate it," Jordan says. "We also want to know whether they represent five people or 5 million people." Many of the groups just want to be heard, he notes, and in turn, Coca-Cola can be heard by them. "If you sit down and talk with them, maybe they can understand what we're trying to do. If you just tell them to go to hell, they'll never understand." Jordan adds that the corporate foundation, in addition to supporting the regional units such as his, also has national areas of focus, notably education and youth. "We've tried to pull out the environmental issues, which are better handled on a local basis, and deal with them, while we leave education and youth to the foundation."

Sticking With Tradition

Traditional corporate philanthropy, if there is such a thing, typically grew up around the conviction of a founder/CEO that the company needed to give something back. The founder/CEO also was usually energized by a favorite cause, as Andrew Carnegie was with libraries or as John D. Rockefeller was with medical research. As companies mature, they often enlist their employees to help them decide where they should give, not just by doing matches, but by directing the lion's share of grants to causes that employees deem beneficial. A third motivator can be reaction to disasters or other serious problems within the corporation's designated community. For example, after 9/11, many companies found ways to donate funds or enlist resources to aid those affected by the disaster. When an earthquake ravages California or a hurricane hits Florida, local corporations will be there to help. All of these rather wide-ranging efforts would fall under the aegis of non-strategic philanthropy because they're not specifically aligned with a company's business goals (except, perhaps, to generate goodwill among employees and stakeholders). Two companies that have not yet gone "strategic" with most of their philanthropy are General Motors Corporation and Adobe Systems, Inc.

General Motors Corporation

"Unlike a lot of companies, we aren't focused," says Rod Gillum, chairman of the General Motors Foundation and vice president for corporate responsibility and diversity for the corporation, which gives away, on average, $50 million annually. "The areas we've been involved in have been historical," including healthcare, K-12 education, and community relations. For example, GM has awarded prizes for 25 years in the area of cancer research. In 2003, it presented three scientists with $250,000 each in recognition of their work. Over the years, the company has awarded nearly $13 million to 101 scientists in an effort to focus worldwide scientific and public attention on cancer research. Part of that stems from GM's huge retiree population and 320,000-person employee base. In the year preceding the 2003 awards, more than 11,000 employees, retirees, and their family members were treated for cancer. "If you talk about strategic philanthropy in the sense of getting people feeling good about the company, the work we've done with the cancer awards is strategic," he says, while acknowledging it does not fit the Kramer/Porter definition. Other causes in which GM has been active include child safety initiatives, campaigns against drunk driving, and environmental activities. It also provides disaster relief and rebuilding aid through GM Global Aid.

"It's not because of a lack of discussion that we're not strategic," says Gillum. "We're always looking at it in some sense." For instance, GM mobilizes vehicles for transportation needs to support charitable initiatives. At a 2002 conference on sustainable development in South Africa, the company donated ambulances for people who needed AIDS drugs. After 9/11, the company gave new trucks to the New York Fire Department. GM has also gotten involved in environmental education tied to the use of fuel cells, which many consider the future of automobile engines. Like Coca-Cola, GM is trying to get environmental groups on board, including the Sierra Club and the Union of Concerned Scientists. But, at the same time, the automaker doesn't want to narrow its options. Says Gillum, "We prefer to be more flexible with our philanthropy, leave the door open." He doesn't believe that philanthropy should be completely self-serving. "Our goals aren't necessarily aligned with the GM corporate mission," he says. "After all, it is supposed to be charity."

Adobe Systems, Inc.

Started in 1982 by John Warnock and Charles Geschke, who remain cochairmen of the board, Adobe harks back to its founders in its philanthropic approach. "John and Chuck had strong values about how the company should be run," says Dyanne Compton, senior manager of worldwide community relations. One of those values is community involvement—to be a model corporate citizen by supporting charitable causes and employee volunteerism. "From the very beginning there was grassroots philanthropy," says Compton, who has been with the company for 15 years. "John and Chuck volunteered themselves." In the 1990s, as Adobe grew, its philanthropic structure got more formal and was put under the community relations heading. The stated mission today is to provide options for underserved populations to more fully participate in the economy. Although that might not help the Silicon Valley company sell more desktop publishing software, it's strategic in the long-term sense, Compton believes. "If we didn't believe this was good for the company, we wouldn't spend our money on it. We use this as a vehicle to enhance Adobe's reputation as a socially responsible corporation and to attract and retain employees."

Strategic or Not?

The fact is, no corporate philanthropy is totally strategic or totally pure. It's more a matter of degree than clear-cut boundaries, as Kramer himself acknowledges. "In the long term, the positioning of a business is dependent on the social context in which it operates," he says. "Social factors in the environment are affected by philanthropy," such as the quality of schools. The idea of strategic philanthropy, he says, is to positively affect both your business and your community with the same initiative. Good strategic philanthropy uses the resources of the corporation to achieve the biggest bang for the buck. While Avon Corporation's work on breast cancer certainly has societal value, "it doesn't necessarily create value for the corporation, because it's not their area of expertise," Kramer says. Corporations need to pick a problem "where they can actually make a difference, not just throw money into the stream with everybody else." Pfizer was able to do that with river blindness, where its research expertise developed a drug to solve the problem. "We think there should be a business benefit of philanthropy, at least with public companies, because they're using shareholder dollars," Kramer says. "So pick a problem that the company can take ownership of and solve." Susan Colby, a partner with Bridgespan, largely agrees with Kramer. "Your reason for existing, as a public company, is shareholder value," she says. "If your source of funds is the corporation, it's very difficult not to be connected to the corporate goal."

But other experts say the picture is fuzzier than Kramer paints it. "Everyone would love giving to be rationally aligned, with some clear way to determine need and get those with resources to share with those in need," says Dinah Waldsmith, senior manager at Business for Social Responsibility, a nonprofit consulting firm. "Instead, you have the messy reality of human beings in political systems trying to determine need and meet it." She adds, "There's lots of room for improvement in the foundation world, but lecturing is not the way to get there." David Vidal, director of research for The Conference Board, maintains that whether philanthropy confers competitive advantage is irrelevant. Kramer and Porter, he suggests, "are trying to fit a square peg into a round hole. They're assuming that the same marketplace factors are in place in corporate philanthropy [as in business], and they aren't." Corporate philanthropy, Vidal adds, operates at the discretion of the corporation, so it will never be standardized. "Who cares what the motivation [for corporate philanthropy] is?" asks David Fetterman, a Stanford University professor and evaluation specialist who's working with Hewlett-Packard on its e-inclusion initiatives. "Companies give out money because they want to look good. So what? I'm not seeing the downside here."

Fetterman has a point. Whether it's Avon going door to door to raise money for breast cancer or Microsoft putting its software in libraries, companies (or people, for that matter) don't do anything out of unadulterated altruism. They do it because they figure it will help them in some way. However, the spirit of helping the community should permeate corporate philanthropy, even when it is predicated on business goals. Considering those goals when drafting a philanthropic mission can be useful in allowing the company to utilize its resources in the most effective manner. Human needs are seemingly endless, so any corporation has to find some method of picking its spots. Going with "strategic philanthropy" can be one of those methods, although it's not the only one.

Tackling the Big Project

In 2000, when Hewlett-Packard Company kicked off its first "Digital Village" in East Palo Alto, California, President Bill Clinton and the Reverend Jesse Jackson, Sr., showed up in person. Three years later, as the project wound down, Jackson again made a personal appearance, while Clinton sent his remarks in writing. Both spoke of the need to give impoverished minority communities, such as East Palo Alto, the tools they needed to compete fairly. "The great challenge of America today is to give kids all those [other] opportunities like it does in the athletic field," Jackson told the largely African-American crowd at the East Palo Alto City Hall. "We do well whenever the playing field is even and the rules are public and the goals are clear. We can make it. The playing field has been uneven in the digital divide….Our mission was launched to even the playing field." As the project was being considered, Jackson met with HP CEO Carly Fiorina. "I told her, 'you have money and technology infrastructure and know-how,'" Jackson recalled. "'We have a market, talent, and location. We both have something of value. We put it together and you have growth. Everybody wins.'"

Putting corporate expertise and resources behind energetic community leadership has become the new recipe for helping to solve some of society's biggest problems, such as poverty, unequal education, and homelessness. Most corporate philanthropy programs are reluctant to take on anything too overwhelming out of fear that they won't be able to make an impact and will just get lost in the crowd. But a few companies have been willing and able to tackle massive, multiyear projects that require serious commitments of money, people, and other resources. Although in other places in this book we've emphasized how small companies can make meaningful contributions, big projects are where big companies can truly shine. Because they have not only the dollars, but also the in-house people power to make a difference. Thus, HP lends its Digital Village partners full-time personnel for three years to help manage and coordinate the projects aimed at empowering poor communities with technology and training. IBM detaches consultants and programmers to work with school districts in "Reinventing Education." Levi Strauss & Company spends a decade working with several rural communities in the United States to combat racism in "Project Change."

These are not problems that lend themselves to quick-and-ready solutions, and, for companies that get involved, require much more than dashing off a check for a single-year grant. Levi initially thought that Project Change would last only five years and cost about $3 million for three sites; it actually took 10 years and $8.4 million (expanding to four sites) before "we started to see meaningful change near the end," says Theresa Fay-Bustillos, executive director of the Levi Strauss Foundation. In this chapter we look at the efforts of HP, IBM, and Levi in undertaking philanthropic projects across different geographic areas in an attempt to ameliorate deep-seated societal problems that most people would consider unsolvable.

Hewlett-Packard Company/Digital Village

In the previous chapter, we described how HP decided to focus its philanthropic giving on select strategic areas that complemented the company's business goals, including education and what it terms "e-inclusion," bridging the digital divide. Under e-inclusion, the Digital Village projects apply the collective force of HP resources, including cash, people, and technology donations, to underserved communities, such as East Palo Alto, Baltimore, and the Tribal Community of Southern California. Digital Villages also expanded globally in 2002 to communities in South Africa, Ghana, and an immigrant section of Paris where the unemployment rate is 30 percent. "Digital Villages were our first major holistic projects," says Debra Dunn, senior vice president of corporate affairs. "The biggest contribution came from the people we put full-time on the ground." In each Digital Village, HP appoints an e-inclusion executive to manage planning and execution. "In business, we develop expertise in goal-setting and prioritizing," notes Dunn. "Those capabilities are extremely valuable in getting things done." Another resource that HP contributes is its connections, such as getting Jesse Jackson and Bill Clinton out to showcase the first Digital Village. "For me it's often picking up the phone, calling someone, and getting them involved," says Dunn.

Describing Digital Village is not a simple matter. For the East Palo Alto Digital Village (EPADV), launched in April 2000, HP committed $5 million in grants and in-kind gifts over three years. The initiatives included community networking through establishment of online resource centers, technology access points, and micro-grants to small nonprofits to enhance their technology capabilities; e-learning through donation of laptop computers for use by students and teachers at the local Belle Haven School; small business development to provide training, capital, and other assistance to aid entrepreneurs in starting up small businesses; and community academy, a state-of-the-art employment and skills-training facility that houses community organizations. Three technology access points were set up, encompassing a senior center, an affordable housing complex, and a community-based rehabilitation and recovery center. EPADV also provided technology tools, including computers, software, and networking equipment, to 30 nonprofits, expanding their service capability. The small business arm delivered equipment and training resources to 70 licensed small business owners and partnered with a nonprofit organization called Start Up, which provides services to help individuals start their own businesses. These efforts have translated into 156 jobs and $2.75 million worth of business for East Palo Alto, according to HP.

"The new approach equals working more collaboratively to address a broader set of issues in underserved communities," says Bess McDowell Stephens, HP's vice president of philanthropy and education. "It's not just making a grant but helping them tackle intractable problems. It's focused on helping communities who have not had access create a vision of what the future would be for their community in conjunction with use of technology." She says, echoing other experts, that throwing technology at communities does not, by itself, solve problems. "It's very difficult for them to anticipate how technology will add value to their lives," without guidance and support in making use of that technology. "It's a natural extension of our work to help integrate technology into living, in homes and schools and the workplace," sums up Stephens.

At the April 29, 2003, event that celebrated the completion of the three-year Digital Village project, community leaders congratulated HP for the company's support and pondered the next steps. "HP put its heart into its [philanthropic] work and did something different," says Rebecca Matthews, chair of the EPADV Advisory Board. "It came to East Palo Alto. No other Fortune 500 company came to East Palo Alto." Indeed, East Palo Alto is a reflection of the deep divide that still exists between the "haves" and "have-nots" in U.S. society, especially in a place such as the San Francisco Bay Area. Part of Silicon Valley, but separated from more upscale communities such as Palo Alto (head-quarters of HP) and Menlo Park by a major freeway, East Palo Alto was originally home to lower-income people, African-Americans and later Pacific Islanders, who began providing needed services to wealthy Santa Clara Valley residents before the name *Silicon Valley* was ever coined. The existence of East Palo Alto, with its rundown housing, high unemployment, and trailing schools, was a painful contrast to the newfound riches generated by the technology revolution. Across the freeway lies one of the highest concentrations of wealth ever created; entrepreneurs and venture capitalists used their money to buy fast cars, fast planes, and second and third vacation homes. They brought in skilled immigrants who could write code—from India, Asia, and Israel—as quickly as the visas could be churned out. But East Palo Also residents, lacking in technology access and skills, did not share in the region's prosperity. HP aimed to change that, and the three-year Digital Village is a tremendous step forward.

"HP gave us the first corporate grant to establish technology infra-structure," says Faye McNair-Knox, executive director of Start Up. "That's so important in a community like East Palo Alto, where we often dream without the resources." HP did not act like a typical donor. "HP likes to roll up its sleeves, sit down at the table, and converse with you as an equal partner," she says. "They're a stakeholder in the process too." Going forward, she says the community wants to continue to partner with HP. "We very much want you to stay at the table with us," she says. "This community is a good place to invest, and Digital Village is the beginning of a long-term model that can be replicated elsewhere." Dunn promised that HP won't pull out now that the formal project is ended. "You're our neighbor," she told the audience of about 100 program participants and graduates. "This is certainly not the end of our relationship with our neighbor." The aim of EPADV was not just to bolster one community, "but about linking together various communities so you can help each other and continue to evolve." When HP started the project, "it was a risky venture on both sides," Dunn says. "We didn't have the complete roadmap. We thought it was an opportunity to learn a new approach together."

In Southern California, HP and the Tribal Community are applying that approach to 18 Native American tribes dispersed across 150 miles in San Diego County. One project was to set up a wireless network to allow all the tribes to communicate and coordinate activities, provide emergency services, and deal with environmental issues. A second initiative established a Website to help tribes preserve and share their languages. In the local schools, HP funded cultural resource centers with Native American themes so that Native Americans and non-Native Americans could learn about that culture. HP also partnered with the Tribal Community to open a digital printing operation that provides jobs, a source of income, and a center for training in high-tech skills. As with East Palo Alto, HP again committed $5 million in cash and donations over the three-year project, which ended in 2004. "One unique thing about HP was that they assigned a full-time administrator to work on-site with us," says Jack Ward, director of human resources and support services for the Tribal Community. "It's very unusual for a funding agency to have a full-time person who works on a daily basis with you for three years." And HP didn't help just with technology planning, but with management and organization, he adds. "Overall they did a wonderful job," Ward says. "They changed the paradigm on how Native Americans are using technology. Until it is something you can integrate into your lives, it's not real. Now it's real." In addition, HP's commitment will help draw other grant-makers to the area. "We're already doing applications for grants online, which we couldn't do before," says Ward. HP gained something too. Because the tribes are in rural areas and function as their own governments, HP gained valuable experience in how to expand the Digital Village concept outside urban areas. "We provided a microcosm of dealing with sovereign nations," he says.

HP has expanded the notion of e-inclusion to Kuppam, India, where it has funded an initiative that includes public-private partnerships to accelerate economic development through the application of technology. The initiative also opens new markets for HP and allows it to try out new products and services. Kuppam acts as a "living lab" for HP to introduce technology solutions and refine them, as in helping local entrepreneurs to build community information centers where residents can tap into on-line government services. This is based on methods HP uses in-house in developing new products. The Kuppam project, along with those in the Digital Villages, actively demonstrates the company's effort to fuse its global-citizenship strategy and its business strategy. "Philanthropy is important to Hewlett-Packard, but we at HP want our contribution and involvement in global-citizenship initiatives to have a far greater impact than simply writing a check would," says Dunn.[1]

IBM Corporation/Reinventing Education

As noted in Chapter 7, IBM has spent $75 million on Reinventing Education (RE) since the program was launched in 1994. Much of that has been in grants to selected school districts and states that survived the rigorous application process. Stan Litow, president of the IBM Foundation, says the whole idea is to use the districts and states that get grants as pilot projects in developing tools and strategies that can be exported elsewhere. RE has provided $2-million grants to 22 U.S. locations, serving more than 10 million students across six states and 15 school districts. It has also expanded to nine countries, including Peru, Mexico, Australia, Brazil, Ireland, Italy, Singapore, the United Kingdom, Vietnam, and Australia. "With Reinventing Education, we chose a project that everybody really wants to be involved in, and then we used a business model to do it," says Janet Rocco, IBM's Northwest region manager for corporate community relations. IBM signs a consulting agreement with each district or state, setting out the goals and what each side is expected to contribute.

"When you say you're doing systemic education reform, you're not just talking about an after-school program," Rocco says. "You're talking about longer-term objectives like increasing student performance." The first two rounds of grants concentrated on developing processes; the third round will work on connecting schools so that they can help each other.

"We're satisfied that we've made enormous amount of progress and done things that have actually impacted student achievement and learning," says Litow. This encompasses tools that enable teachers to learn more effectively, make better use of technology, improve assessment of student performance, and provide higher-quality assistance to at-risk kids. "In IBM research labs they turned out a suite of those tools that stand the test," he adds. "If you were evaluating this in a business sense, you'd say being able to lay out some specific goals and meet them over a long period of time means we've had a good track record." Reinventing Education "has actually resulted in specific student achievement gains on a broad scale," Litow says. While other education philanthropy has done that with single schools, "no one that I know of has done it with the size and scale and sustainability that we have." For example, in West Virginia, teachers are using IBM Learning Village, an online communications and collaboration network, to design instructional activities in academic areas where students need the most help. Some 1,700 teachers in that state have been trained on Learning Village, which has now been expanded to Memphis, Tennessee; North Carolina; and San Francisco. In a measurement of teacher technology skills, 90 percent in West Virginia increased their scores. At the same time, students in grades 7–11 in the state saw their scores on the Stanford Achievement Test measurably increase.

A three-year study by an outside agency, Education Development Center, Inc., concluded that IBM's Reinventing Education program has produced a range of school improvements, including significant performance gains for students in grades 7–11. The initiative has also helped states and school districts strengthen teaching skills and improve school organization and management, according to the report. "This report confirms that technology can be a critical component of education reform—when it is used strategically," says Bob Spielvogel, principal author of the study, which was produced by EDC's Center for Children and Technology, in New York. "Reinventing Education goes far beyond technology and engages researchers, corporate managers, and educators in a long-term partnership committed to serious sustained collaboration to improve schools. This makes it unique among the efforts to reform education." The report concludes that RE helped states and districts to establish effective programs for teacher professional development, implement programs that will serve as best practice models for other schools, and sustain momentum even after the grant expired. IBM solutions "have woven themselves into the fabric of everyday school life, and continue to be expanded and inspire new investments beyond the life of the IBM grant."

For a microcosm of how the IBM program works, we talked to Dana Serleff, president and CEO of the Every Child Can Learn Foundation (ECCLF) in San Francisco. In partnership with the San Francisco School District, ECCLF administered a $2-million, five-year RE grant awarded in 1997. "At the outset, IBM asked school districts to propose things they wanted to change with technology," recalls Serleff. "IBM was not crafting the solution. I like that a lot about the program. It's made it easier to keep the project going through multiple leadership levels." What San Francisco wanted was a workflow tool to automate the process by which teachers referred at-risk students to what were called student support teams (SSTs). The idea of the SST was to help the students work out issues without having to be taken out of their mainstream classes. But what was happening was that minority students, African-Americans and Latinos, were being over-referred to special education rather than the SSTs. IBM developed a software tool to automate the SST process. "This tool helps the teacher brainstorm with the problems and track what's working and what's not working," says Serleff. It also gives the school system information on what problems teachers are taking to the SST. "IBM provided the base for building the tool, the software designers to help build the tool, and money for computers to start rolling it out," says Serleff. "We field tested it."

In 2003, ECCLF was dispatching the tool to elementary schools in San Francisco. The expectation is that issues can be resolved by SSTs before a child goes to special education. "We haven't set specific benchmarks, but we want to see an improvement," says Serleff. "The idea is to start with the most basic level of intervention before you make the drastic move to special education." She says teachers have responded positively to the change, because it's much more streamlined to enter data into the computer than filling out a three-page report. Also, the teacher can review the student's record by accessing it on a PC rather than searching for a paper record in a folder. "In the old, manual system, the paper records got lost," and teachers had to refile information each time a student had a problem. Serleff says she liked the fact that IBM would let the district try different approaches and retrench, if need be. She also appreciated attending the IBM-sponsored education conferences and exchanging ideas with other grantees. Litow adds that the first tool IBM developed for San Francisco proved to be too complex. "We thought we were going to build a set of tools to provide a new vehicle for people to communicate around a particular special education case," he says. What proved to be more effective "was a simpler set of tools that gave people access to a common set of information about kids." He adds, "If you're smart enough to listen to people at the ground level, you can switch and become more effective." Education customers are just like IBM's business customers. "You have to understand what they're trying to do and not have a preconceived notion about what's going to work," says Litow.

Levi Strauss Foundation/Project Change

In 1991, Levi Strauss ventured where almost no other companies had gone before: It funded a multimillion-dollar initiative designed to address racial bias and institutional racism in four rural communities in the United States where the company had a presence. Seeing the initiative through took twice the amount of time (10 years) that Levi had originally envisioned and more than twice the amount of cash ($8.4 million). The overarching goal of Project Change was to create a core of community members of different races and professions to develop a plan to openly address racism, both in people and in key institutions of the communities. The first three sites were El Paso, Texas; Valdosta, Georgia; and Albuquerque, New Mexico. In 1993, Knoxville, Tennessee, was added as a fourth site. Theresa Fay-Bustillos, executive director of the Levi Strauss Foundation, says even though Levi has refocused its philanthropic efforts since Project Change, the effort, nonetheless, was in keeping with the company's philosophy. "We want to tear down barriers," she says. "A lot of what we do is dictated by our pioneering spirit. If you look at all our history of corporate social responsibility, there's a theme of addressing social barriers." At the end of the 1980s, when Levi was doing very well financially, it gave the foundation a special onetime gift of $3 million "to make a difference on an important social issue," she remembers. Out of many proposals, "the idea of addressing racism in rural communities where we operated manufacturing plants was particularly meaningful and interesting." Fay-Bustillos says that interest hearkened back "to the courageous stand the company took in 1960 when it insisted that the manufacturing plant it was opening in Blackstone, Virginia, be a racially integrated facility," years before the landmark 1964 Civil Rights Act.

The first step of Project Change was to recruit voluntary task forces composed of business, government, and community leaders in each community, the majority of whom were women and people of color. Each task force held a two-day retreat to receive training on how to develop a common framework on combating racism. Levi provided ongoing technical assistance in creating community change, building coalitions, working with local media, developing strategic plans, and creating effective teams. Then each task force developed three-year action plans to address the four goals of the project: dismantling institutional policies and practices that promote racial discrimination, easing tensions between different groups, promoting diversity in the leadership of community institutions, and preventing overt acts of racial and cultural prejudice. Levi committed to fund the project initially for up to five years, as long as adequate progress was made, according to Fay-Bustillos, but the task proved so challenging that the time period had to be extended. "Racism in rural communities in the South and Southwest was very entrenched and institutionalized," she says. "We actually started off thinking the project would last five years and we would spend about $3 to $4 million." However, as the five-year mark approached, "we realized that we were just starting to make progress on such an entrenched social ill." The progress was definable enough, though, that Levi renewed its commitment. "Members of all races and ethnicities were actually coming together to talk about race and racism in ways they had never done before and were busy volunteering their time to challenge the racism undermining their communities," recalls Fay-Bustillos. "So, how could we pull the plug at that point? We began thinking instead about how we could sustain our longer-term involvement."

To that end, in 1997, Levi transferred oversight of Project Change to the Tides Foundation. The idea, says Fay-Bustillos, was to enable a permanent structure that could obtain support from other foundations. On a national basis, she says, Project Change has set up an online Anti-Racism Network (*www.antiracismnet.org*) to serve as a clearinghouse for resources and training. "We realized that if the local sites were to realize their potential, they would need a full-time director and supervision," she says. The national Project Change organization still operates under the leadership of a director who was brought in by the Levi Strauss Foundation, Shirley Strong. For several more years after 1997, "the Levi Strauss Foundation continued to be the sole funder, but we set up clear expectations about results and a schedule for decreasing funding over time," Fay-Bustillos says. She adds that Project Change "showed us that we cannot ignore racism—it has not gone away and continues to undermine the work of community-building and our future as a society," which is why Levi determined that the effort needed to be taken over by a national organization.

After the 10 years, Levi could point to a number of concrete accomplishments that indicated progress. These included:

▶ **In Albuquerque:** creation of the Fair Lending Center at the University of New Mexico, which helps people of color obtain loans; establishment of the Anti-Racism Training Institute to build coalitions of people interested in reforming key institutions; establishment of a predatory lending task force to draft legislation to eliminate this practice—the Home Loan Protection Act was signed by the governor in April 2003.

▶ **In Valdosta:** creation of a micro-enterprise Loan Pool Program to fund small businesses and provide outreach to clients who have little access to funding; creation of the Homebuyer Education and Home Loan Pool Program to assist nontraditional bank customers in purchasing homes; establishment of Amigos to serve the needs of non-English speaking residents as they seek healthcare, legal, and other services.

> ▶ **In Knoxville:** creation of the Hate Crimes Working Group, a collaboration with law enforcement to raise awareness about hate crimes; development of the Center for Race and Community Building, which offers anti-racism training, resources, and other services for a nine-county area.

> ▶ **In El Paso:** creation of the Hate Crimes Task Force to address law enforcement along the Texas/Mexico border and to look into racial profiling issues.

Several important lessons came out of the experience with Project Change. "You must set clear goals and be focused," Fay-Bustillos says. Otherwise, "the community will expect you to address each and every incident involving allegations of race—and you can't." She also says you must get local people involved, not depend on outsiders for leadership. "You need to build a core group of local leaders committed to addressing racism," and that core group has to include influential institutional players as well as consumers. And, of course, it must be racially and ethnically diverse. Although local personnel from the Levi Strauss Foundation served on the task forces, "we were not seen as independent, but invested with our local grantees," she says. However, she adds, the task forces do need "professional expertise" to tackle racism; "without it they made little progress." If she were to start the project today, she would build in more cross-site collaboration, especially on issues such as how to get community support for creating change. "The extent of community ownership was directly related to the credibility of the local task forces and whether some tangible results were achieved," Fay-Bustillos says. "Project Change taught us that you need partnerships and leadership from business, the nonprofits, and community-based organizations (including churches), and from local government, to make real progress on an issue so embedded into our social fabric and institutions." Although former President Clinton gave Levi the first Ron Brown Award for Project Change, a very "proud moment" for the corporation, "in truth, there was no one event that signaled success to us," says Fay-Bustillos, "but many small changes that began to add up and make us realize our commitment had been worth it in the end."

The Big Project Requirements

1. Multiyear commitment of resources.

2. Dedicated, paid staff to manage the project.

3. Partnerships with key nonprofit and government players.

4. Diversity of leadership and participants.

5. Establishment of clear, mutually beneficial goals.

6. Networking with other experts and funders.

7. Defining and examining the core problems (rather than merely symptoms) to address.

8. Sustainability planning.

9. External evaluation by a respected third party.

10. Flexibility and innovation in responding to bumps along the road.

Keeping Hope Alive

The previous examples show that corporations can indeed make a difference in addressing deep-rooted, seemingly insolvable societal problems. To be sure, Levi's efforts are not going to eliminate racism; IBM won't reinvent education in every location that needs it; nor will HP succeed in totally eliminating the digital divide. Still, these companies' efforts provide a pattern for how corporations can undertake major, multiyear philanthropic efforts and deliver definitive progress. Some of the commonalities in these efforts include willingness to devote significant resources over a long-term period; participation of key people within the corporation, both in advocating for the projects and in staffing them; strong partnerships and two-way communication with nonprofits that will be involved in the work; flexibility in readjusting priorities and methods;

and, above all, the belief that meaningful change is possible. As Confucius supposedly said, "A journey of a thousand miles begins with a single step." If we throw up our hands and say some problems are too big for anyone to solve, we'll never get there. At least Levi, IBM, HP, and other companies that undertake these kinds of efforts are willing to get some skin in the game.

And the payoffs come at celebrations such as HP's Digital Village party at East Palo Alto City Hall. About 150 people filled the room, snacking on hors d'oeuvres supplied by one of the new small businesses spun out of Start Up. In front, a reggae band played next to a pyramid of boxes bearing the HP and Compaq brand names. Women in dreadlocks and colorful prints pressed the hands of HP executives in tailored suits. Junior-high students showed off the video they made of how their classwork got more engaging as a result of the laptops HP donated to their school. And Jesse Jackson preached in the measured cadences of a revival meeting: "Today there's joy in this place. The brains were already here. The talent was already here. We needed access and opportunity, and you gave us that. Keep hope alive." The crowd enthusiastically echoed him. "We've begun the process, run a long way, and we have a long way to go," summed up Regina Thompson, project lead coordinator. "We want to make very, very certain that next year's Digital Village will be even more fruitful than our first three years."

Good Partners Make
Good Philanthropy

Previously in this book, we've concentrated on what corporations can do internally to achieve best practices in philanthropy. Here, and in the following three chapters, we explore the role of partners, intermediaries, and other external groups in influencing corporate philanthropy. The importance of forging good partnerships cannot be overestimated. Corporations that think they can simply dive into the nonprofit world with the same techniques and timetables that they've used successfully in the business world can find themselves sadly disillusioned. For one thing, as noted in Chapter 10, many of the issues with which nonprofits are wrestling are the biggest conundrums we face as a society: homelessness, poverty, discrimination, lack of access to healthcare or other services. These do not lend themselves to quick fixes or a onetime infusion of cash. "Everyone is always looking for the silver bullet, with the idea that you're going to fix something in two or three years when it took generations to create this mess," says David Fetterman, a Stanford University faculty member who is teaming with Hewlett-Packard to evaluate its Digital Village project. "I'm not against short-term wins, but it often takes a long-term approach to build the capacity to solve real problems."

Before they can be effective philanthropists, corporations need to build their own capacity for community service. Of course, this means hiring effective people internally to run the foundation or corporate giving organization, but it also means finding effective partners in the nonprofit world. Many of the examples highlighted in this book involve strong alliances between corporations and nonprofits, such as LensCrafters and Lions Clubs International, in donating eyeglasses to the Third World; Starbucks and Conservation International, in encouraging coffee growers to use environmentally sustainable practices; or Levi Strauss and the Asia Foundation, in reaching out to overseas workers. Corporate philanthropy, in fact, requires managing a multitude of partnerships—some very localized; others national in scope. In the best partnerships, both sides give and get. Typically, the corporation contributes funding, personnel, and expertise in planning and prioritizing. The nonprofit partner provides opportunities to do good and advice as to how to apply these corporate resources.

As with any relationship, it's a two-way street. The biggest complaint that nonprofits have about corporations (see Chapter 14) is that they rush in thinking they know how to do it all in the nonprofit world. Then the corporations get frustrated when there's a disconnect between their timetable and what's happening in the nonprofit world, and back off. But those corporations that take the time to build up partnerships with nonprofits and listen to their input are far more effective and less likely to run into brick walls. In this chapter, we take a look at three examples of national partnerships—one just getting started, one several years old, and one long-standing—and consider how they're structured, the key success factors, and what each side brings to the table.

eBay, Inc./MissionFish

From the start, eBay's philanthropy has used intermediaries (see next chapter) and only recently, in 2002, became a full-fledged corporate foundation with an individualized mission. Irene Wong, executive director of the foundation, says that eBay basically wants to empower communities to make positive changes. One way to do that is to leverage eBay's unique business model—online auctions—into the nonprofit world. Early on, eBay incorporated a charity fund-raising page within its site, where nonprofits can describe their missions and conduct auctions, Wong says. After September 11, 2001, eBay did an Auction for America that raised $10 million to help victims of the tragedy.

Through that effort came feedback from users that they'd like to see more charitable auctions from eBay. So the company has aligned itself with MissionFish, a Washington, D.C.-based nonprofit affiliated with the Points of Light Foundation, which specializes in charity auctions. "By teaming with MissionFish, our users will be able to earmark a specific portion of their proceeds to charity," Wong explains. MissionFish will be the middleman, hosted on the eBay site. Those who are selling there will have a special icon to indicate proceeds are going to charity.

Sean Milliken, the president and CEO of MissionFish, says he and several others with nonprofit consulting experience started the organization in late 2000. "It was based on my personal frustration with nonprofits being unable to expand their services because of a lack of funding," he says, particularly so-called *unrestricted funding* that can be used for administrative functions and capacity building. In addition, "we recognized there was an untapped resource called in-kind gifts," although some nonprofits joke that these are "unkind gifts" because they don't always match the organization's need, but simply provide a nifty tax write-off for the donor. When Milliken worked at the Boys & Girls Clubs, "I would get daily calls on everything from a truckload of basketballs to a warehouse of computers that someone wanted to donate," he says. "The process of storing those goods and trying to redistribute them was a problem." Milliken concluded that most nonprofits would rather have the money than the actual goods, so he created MissionFish to link donors and buyers. "Our system creates an auction offering and identifies the highest bidder," he says, thereby allowing the nonprofit to turn, say, donated computers or shoes or whatever into money.

But because MissionFish was a new, unknown Website, it did not attract the kind of traffic Milliken wanted. Hence, he turned to eBay and its community of 62 million users. "We wanted to link donors and buyers with no administration costs for nonprofits," he says. Often, though, would-be donors have not learned how to use the eBay system. So MissionFish steps in to enable donors to easily access eBay's worldwide trading community. Nonprofits interested in benefiting from the eBay marketplace must register with MissionFish. Then, sellers who use eBay are offered the opportunity to donate a percentage of their proceeds (anywhere from 20 to 100 percent) to charity. The sellers pick from the registered nonprofits that they want the donation to go to, and their goods appear on eBay with a charity icon so that buyers know some of their proceeds will be used for nonprofits. Once the auction concludes, MissionFish collects the charitable percentage from the seller, deducts a small fee (in most cases, $2.50 per item), and distributes the rest to the selected nonprofits, providing the seller with a tax receipt. Nonprofits can also direct donors to the site.

With MissionFish, "we have created new sources of revenue for nonprofits, but we have not engaged millions of people," says Milliken. "We see that vision becoming reality because eBay has embraced our model." The MissionFish site was launched in the fall of 2003 on eBay at *www.ebay.com/givingworks/*. By the fifth year of the agreement, he expects, conservatively, to distribute $20 million annually to nonprofits as a result of eBay auctions in which the seller agrees to donate a portion to charity. By contrast, in three years on its own, MissionFish raised about $400,000. "To be candid, we have not met our goals," Milliken acknowledges. "We believe we can do that by leveraging eBay." (MissionFish has also leveraged salesforce.com, whose software is running the back end of the auction project.)

What MissionFish brings to eBay is experience with the nonprofit world. "One of our primary responsibilities is to vet the nonprofits who register with us and make sure that they're legitimate," says Milliken. MissionFish also will carry insurance to guarantee that the nonprofit will get paid. "We owe it to our nonprofits and communities we live in to be more creative about raising funds," he says. By allying with eBay, "we can leverage what they do best with what we do best, to create a whole new source of revenue." Hopefully, this will make nonprofits less dependent on ongoing fund-raising and more able to plan ahead. With eBay's help, "we can teach nonprofits how to build fisheries," Milliken concludes.

Microsoft Corporation/NPower

In 1999, a group of prestigious corporations, including Microsoft and Boeing, that did grantmaking in the Seattle area got together and commissioned consultant Joan Fanning to do a study on how nonprofits could use technology more effectively. Microsoft then asked Fanning to write a business plan, which evolved into NPower. "The main emphasis of NPower is to provide humanware that understood technology, understood nonprofits, and could help them implement it," says Fanning, now the executive director of NPower. In surveys she did of nonprofits, the main barrier was not obtaining hardware or software, but finding "the know-how and hands-on assistance," she recalls. Jane Meseck, manager of community affairs for Microsoft, says the company frequently got requests from nonprofits that wanted software donations, but "we were unsure whether it was being implemented effectively." That led to the work with Fanning outlining the gap between what nonprofits needed in the way of technology help and what they were getting. Along with other corporate funders, Microsoft contributed $250,000 annually for three years to get NPower up and running in Seattle. NPower, which has now morphed into a federation of 12 local organizations in different cities, employs staff consultants who will distribute donated technology and do technology assessment and training for other nonprofits. It also makes use of corporate volunteers. "We've actually found that most employees from high-tech companies are willing to work on whatever technology we need them to," says Fanning. "I've had volunteers from Microsoft working on Apple computers. They're not political," she emphasizes. "The corporations may be political, but the people who volunteer just want to do good."

However, she praises Microsoft for working very much behind the scenes in getting NPower started. In September 2000, Microsoft embarked on a five-year partnership, powered by a $25-million grant ($10 million in cash and $15 million in software), with NPower to deliver the program to additional locations outside Seattle. Among the cities now served by locally affiliated NPowers are New York, Indianapolis, Detroit, Portland, Atlanta, and San Francisco. "Microsoft did this in a very quiet way," says Fanning. "They did not want to advertise that Microsoft was behind it, because they have such a big footprint. They had the Seattle Community Foundation take a front seat." But Microsoft, which sits on the NPower board, is the primary corporate partner and the moving force behind the nonprofit. "It was because of them we got started at all," says Fanning. "They said, 'we believe in this' and gave us operating funds. They also gave us expertise to help us succeed in drafting a business plan, and they continue to open doors for us." But Microsoft did not want to be the sole funder. With each subsequent NPower the challenge was to encourage local organizations to provide funding and have somebody sit on the board. The Microsoft portion of NPower's total operating budget is now no more than about one-fifth, Fanning estimates. "One thing Microsoft has done a good job of is not focusing on branding power. They've tried to give under the radar, realizing that there is a lot of feeling about the Microsoft name, which can be both good and bad."

Meseck says that the theme of the NPower partnership is "appropriate technology for the nonprofit." Although other corporate funders have joined in the effort (see the following section for an example), Microsoft remains the driver in duplicating the NPower model across the country. "We wanted to look at how we could replicate what was successful in Seattle, as a national funder in local communities, and at the same time ensure they created their own NPowers," she adds. The key success criteria are: community-based, community-designed, and community-supported. "It's not a cookie cutter," Meseck emphasizes. Each NPower "is based on the needs of the community and supported by local nonprofits." In a few cases, communities couldn't get an organization started because the nonprofit applying wasn't a good fit with NPower, she says. Microsoft has worked with NPower to develop evaluations of what has been done locally. "We wanted to develop a pattern for how a national-level funder can be seen as a local partner," says Meseck, while leaving decision-making in the hands of the local group. Microsoft does site visits to the communities, works with local groups to do the start-up and fund-raising, and in some cases, has local Microsoft people sit on the board. "When we made the list of eligible cities, we matched that with our field offices," she says. "NPower national can move just about anywhere."

NPower has expanded its list of national supporters to include other corporate and community foundations. For example, the telecommunications giant SBC Communications, Inc., signed on in 2001. Laura Sanford, president of the SBC Foundation, says NPower's mission dovetailed well with the SBC Excelerator program, which provides grants ($8.5 million in 2003) to assist nonprofits in implementing technology. "SBC Excelerator is our signature program," she says. "We made national grants to organizations we thought could serve as a strong umbrella for what we were trying to do on the local level.

NPower was one of those and has proven to be an extremely capable partner." So far, Sanford says, SBC has given NPower $1.5 million over two years, and anticipates continuing that level of support. Adds Fanning, "The partnership with SBC was building on their core focus: to help nonprofits use technology to better serve their communities." The first project was a small grant to add a section on Internet access to a published NPower document on technology benchmarks for nonprofits. In 2002–3, NPower used the $1.5 million in SBC grants to provide technology capacity-building services to nonprofits in SBC's 13 states of interest. This included leadership training in how to think about, plan, and implement technology, as well as hands-on consulting. As Fanning explains it, "the first project was all about raising the floor, improving the infrastructure." The next series of grants from SBC will be used to "raise the ceiling" by doing a series of technology inspiration summits around the country for nonprofits. The target markets are small to mid-size nonprofits with annual budgets of less than $1.5 million.

Like Microsoft, SBC also provides company volunteers with expertise in Internet access or telecommunications. "They struck a great balance between having a focus area and understanding what worked for them and giving us freedom to establish our mission," says Fanning of SBC. "Whenever you work in an intensive partnership, you have to understand the internal workings and communicate correctly. We serve as a bridge between the reality of corporations and the reality of nonprofits."

Timberland/City Year

Perhaps the epitome of national partnerships is Timberland's long-lasting relationship with City Year, extending back to 1989 with the donation of 50 pairs of boots by then-COO Jeffrey Swartz, who now heads the company as CEO. Swartz serves on the national Board of Trustees for City Year, after acting as its chairman for a decade. During 14 years, Timberland has made more than $20 million in cash and product donations to City Year, which encourages young adults of diverse backgrounds to engage in a year of full-time community service. The corporation also houses the headquarters for City Year New Hampshire.

Although in this book we have defined philanthropy broadly, to include not only cash gifts but also service, Swartz distinguishes between the two. "Our view is that what we've been doing isn't about philanthropy but about redistributing value. The majority of what we do I would characterize as investments in community as opposed to philanthropy," he says. "The brilliance of the City Year model is that you can drive right down the street and find that community."

In 2003, City Year had a presence in 14 metropolitan locations in the United States, with more than 1,000 young adults performing service outfitted in red jackets, khaki pants, and boots from Timberland. The youth corps are a highly visible force for community service, performing functions ranging from serving as teachers' aides, running after-school programs and school vacation camps, teaching the prevention of violence and AIDS, rehabilitating public housing units, and building parks and playgrounds. Corps members receive a weekly stipend and, upon graduating the program, an educational award of $4,725 from the Corporation for National Service. Since its founding in 1988, City Year has engaged more than 6,000 young adults in service; provided more than 10.6 million hours of service to 1,000 nonprofit organizations, schools, and community centers; and generated more than $22 million in post-service scholarships for the young adults who serve. Says Swartz, "Our history with City Year has grown deeper and more dynamic each day, because we are both organizations built on beliefs."

Carolyn Casey, director of social enterprise for Timberland, calls City Year a "cornerstone partner" for Timberland, whose philanthropic mission is to equip people to make a difference in the world. At many Timberland corporate events, including sales meetings, consumer/industry engagement sessions, and diversity and leadership training, City Year provides opportunities for participants to serve the communities where the events are located. Many of the employee volunteer projects include teaming up with City Year. For example, in 2003, Timberland employees joined with City Year New York, the Civilian Conservation Association, the Robin Hood Organization, and a local public school to transform a blacktopped lot into a community garden in New York City. "It's multisector collaboration at its best," says Casey. Adds Swartz, "All our constituents—employees, consumers, shareholders, and the community—benefit from the Timberland/City Year partnership." Sharing community experiences helps employees and executives at Timberland to bond and to improve their skills in team-building and diversity." He notes that City Year staff members participate in many Timberland functions and some alumni of the community service organization have become employees. "Many companies pay thousands upon thousands of dollars for the type of team-building skills we learn through giving of ourselves," Swartz says. "So not only is Timberland furthering positive change and community betterment, we are making an investment in our infrastructure."

Michael Brown, the president and cofounder of Boston-based City Year, calls himself a "social entrepreneur" who wants to meet community needs in creative ways. "We think America needs to encourage young people especially, and we find that many of the same ideas apply about entrepreneurship," he says. Like Swartz, Brown believes that "the highest partnerships between corporations and nonprofits are formed over shared visions and values." The old model of philanthropy—a check in exchange for a PR blurb—is disappearing, Brown maintains. In its place is enlightened self-interest. "Jeff Swartz doesn't want his employees to check half of themselves at the door. People are happier, more productive, and more ethical when you have these partnerships in place." Brown compares a good partnership with a Swiss Army knife, because "it can do so many things at once." He urges corporations that want to do philanthropy to seek out deep partnerships. "You can make one or two big bets instead of scattering dollars here and there," he says. "Your employees can get leadership training in a nonprofit, serving on boards." He agrees with Swartz that 21st-century companies are not just judged on the quality of their products, but the quality of their values.

Timberland also gets a powerful branding opportunity with City Year, Brown points out. "They put a complete toe-to-head uniform on every City Year corpsman across the country. It's good for their brand, and it makes our program cohesive and powerful; it makes the young people feel special." In return, he says, "we try to do whatever Timberland asks of us to come and help them pursue their vision of being a company with service beliefs," including setting up locations in cities where Timberland is planning to open a store. "You try to find opportunities to partner in deeper ways," he says. "Over the years, hundreds of Timberland employees have engaged with our people. We've all seen the strategic value that helps us in what we're trying to do. If they want to try out some new apparel, we can help them. But, most of all, we want to help their civic mission."

Learning from its partnership with Timberland, City Year has now added a number of other national partners, including Cisco, Hewlett-Packard (by virtue of its merger with Compaq), and Comcast. In 1993, San Jose Mayor Susan Hammer asked City Year to come to that Silicon Valley City and brokered a meeting with John Morgridge, then the CEO of Cisco. "He listened to us and said, 'we're in,'" recalls Brown. In 1999, City Year did its national convention in San Jose, and Morgridge spoke. City Year became the first nonprofit to participate in Cisco's Executive Briefing Center, where Fortune 500 companies typically come to learn about technology. "Cisco wants to see the nonprofit world become just as e-savvy as the for-profit world," says Brown. Cisco gave City Year a $1-million grant to get networked and go paperless in paying its team members. City Year was also home to seven of the laid-off Cisco employees who worked in the nonprofit world. Brown says one of the Cisco people glanced over a City Year time sheet and said, "This should be paperless," and helped the nonprofit "build a world-class intranet." Now the two are sharing the vision of "showing nonprofits the way to technology." HP is funding City Year teams in Boston and San Jose, and also sponsoring an annual award to City Year alumni, consisting of an HP Leadership Award and a notebook computer. Comcast, which is moving into new markets with its cable business, has given a $2-million grant "to partner with us around the country," says Brown. Comcast also has sponsored a national public service announcement for the City Year corps. With all these partners, "we're looking for ways where we can share a civic vision and make it happen," he says.

Culture Mesh

As the examples in this chapter have shown, corporations and nonprofits don't have to be locked into an inevitable culture clash—if they can find ways to align their visions and contribute to each other's success. City Year's Brown points out that corporations represent "can-do cultures" that bring needed energy into the nonprofit world, "which has to deal with problems that are so overwhelming, it can make us dour."

However, corporations must be careful not to overstate what they can deliver to nonprofits, and vice versa, he cautions. "If you're working closely with a for-profit entity, you're going to have to work through issues. Don't think of them as just a checkbook. Like any relationship, keep the lines of communication open."

6 Steps to Successful
Corporate/Nonprofit Partnerships

1. Both partners must share visions, values, and goals.

2. Treat the nonprofit as an equal partner, whose opinions and contributions are valued.

3. Even though the partnership may be national, the projects must be community-based, with local input and support.

4. Funding sources should be multiple to assure sustainability.

5. Corporations and nonprofit partners should each provide needed expertise. For example, corporations can teach about prioritizing goals and devising measurement; nonprofits, about meeting diverse needs and utilizing resources effectively.

6. Support should be hands-on, with executives and employees taking an active role in working with the nonprofit partner.

One theme running through a lot of corporate philanthropy these days is "making an impact." Instead of doling out small amounts to multiple projects, corporations want to concentrate on bigger projects that truly make a difference. But generally, this takes partners from the nonprofit world, who are just as visionary. Few corporate executives have much understanding of many issues that confront nonprofits—not just the societal problems they're trying to assuage but also the need to constantly raise money and fund operating expenses along with project-based work. Similarly, nonprofits don't always comprehend the pressures that confront executives of public companies, especially the requirement to balance shareholder demands with community needs. Serving on each other's boards and participating jointly in projects can help corporations and nonprofits to enhance and improve not only their communities, but also themselves.

The Intermediary's Role

Not every corporation wants to go it alone on philanthropy. Beyond the type of partnerships discussed in the previous chapters are so-called intermediaries—nonprofit foundations set up with the express purpose of aggregating corporate (and sometimes individual) donations and "investing" them in community service. Particularly for small companies, there are myriad advantages. Using an intermediary circumvents the need to set up a corporate foundation, with all the attendant legal and accounting requirements. An intermediary probably will not require a full-time person inside the company to deal with it, whereas a corporate foundation or giving program usually does. Companies forego the headache of poring through all the grant requests themselves and hand that off to someone else. For another thing, they get expert advice on philanthropy from an organization familiar with the issues that can serve as a connection point between corporations and community nonprofits, and vet the latter, using various benchmarks. The intermediary can also act as a stepping-stone for small companies that want to get started in philanthropy, learn how to do it, and then initiate their own programs. Besides handling donations, intermediaries can help arrange employee volunteer projects, in-kind giving, and other forms of non-monetary service. Through all this, the intermediary and the company select the goals for the philanthropy, so it's not just tossing money into a pool.

There also can be disadvantages to having an intermediary. Its percentage cut can be up to 50 percent of the dollars contributed. And corporate philanthropy is not as apparent when it's done through, say, Community Foundation Silicon Valley instead of through eBay itself. Some companies like it that way, preferring to remain anonymous and low-key in their giving, but others seek more direct involvement—as in the strategic philanthropy cited in Chapter 9—and greater impact. These companies want to take an active role in managing their community investments and, while public relations is hopefully not the primary goal, certainly it has its place. Publicizing a program can bring in other donors, energize volunteers, and bring warranted attention to nonprofits doing important work. So intermediaries are flexible in how they structure their arrangements with corporations. Some companies write a check and hand it over, leaving everything else in the hands of the intermediary. More typical is an agreement under which the intermediary acts like a consultant to the company, helping it to structure its giving and decide on priorities, then taking care of the "back end" by making grants and doing the accounting. This still allows the company to collect on the PR goodwill.

In this chapter we will consider the role of several different types of intermediaries, including community foundations and entrepreneur foundations. Because this book is devoted to corporate giving, we will not explore what has become known as venture philanthropy, which is primarily utilized by wealthy individuals, although some corporations also contribute. Venture philanthropy applies the techniques of venture capital investing to the nonprofit world, seeking to impose other "businesslike" goals and benchmarks (such as serving a certain number of people, raising school test scores, and the like) in lieu of reaching profitability. It is a model that has fallen somewhat out of favor in the nonprofit world because of its perceived arrogance about applying the rules of business to massive societal ills. Nonetheless, as we'll see in the next chapter, the notions of accountability and definable results are increasingly taking hold in the nonprofit world, so venture philanthropy has had an influence, as have the other types of intermediaries cited here.

Community Foundations

Community foundations, of which there are about 600 in the United States, specialize in a specific geographic area, providing charitable giving advice to companies and individual donors. Take Community Foundation Silicon Valley (CFSV) which, despite its trendy mission statement: "building a stronger community through strategic philanthropy," is no newcomer. It was started in 1954, when Silicon Valley was still the Santa Clara Valley, and has since sprouted like a start-up. From an initial endowment of $55,000, CFSV now manages more than $500 million on behalf of several hundred individuals, families, and corporations. The aptly named Jeff Sunshine, CFSV's corporate services officer, says that in 2003 the foundation added four new corporate programs—Xilinx, Rambus, Intuitive Surgical, and Crystal Decisions—to the 15 it already managed. He says that corporations understand philanthropy from a product standpoint, but not from a resource standpoint. Tapping into a community foundation "enables them to free up resources internally by partnering with someone who understands how communities work," he says. "We're closer to the ground. We understand our community because we have to raise money from it and give it back." Corporations that "don't want to take the heat of saying no" find community foundations attractive, Sunshine adds. "We do all of the backroom operations—set up the initiatives, interface with the nonprofits, get employees involved. They [corporations] don't have to get their hands messy in the same way."

CFSV offers several options to corporations and accepts either cash or stock in payment, although it prefers the former. Unlike the entrepreneurs foundations profiled in the next section, "we don't hold the stock. We sell it immediately," says Sunshine. Under a new model developed by CFSV, corporations will pay an up-front fee—10 percent of the money they'll be donating annually—and CFSV will set up a philanthropic account with the company's money and run it. "Basically, we do your grant-making for you," says Sunshine. Another model is to establish an endowment or seed an ongoing fund through CFSV, but the corporation is more involved in selecting grantees. However, CFSV dispenses the funds. The typical fee is 1 percent a month of the total asset value, which can be significant for a large fund, although "we do some negotiating," says Sunshine. "We've got a staff of 50 and have to cover our costs." A third alternative is a pass-through fund, where the company simply sets up an account with CFSV but directs all the grant-making itself and dispenses the funds. "They keep the money with us because of the tax consequences," he says. There's only a minimal fee for the pass-through. Sometimes "we don't even collect one," Sunshine says. In 2003, the corporate funds were split about evenly between pass-through and endowments; the up-front-fee model was just being introduced.

CFSV can help a corporate philanthropic effort crawl, walk, and then run. Says Sunshine, "We often train the corporate grantmaking staff in how to make a good grant, how to give due diligence, how to make an on-site visit, and how to determine the goals. Meanwhile, we're the one the IRS talks to" about the taxes on the funds. Companies that allow CFSV to select their grantees (called a "corporate-advised fund") work with the foundation to establish a mission. When they go off on their own, "that's brought back to the corporation," he says. For companies and individuals who are just getting their feet wet, CFSV has a Partners in Philanthropy program where they can select from competitive grants that come into the organization, such as a senior center or a school. "For some of the newer organizations, it's very attractive," he says. "They can give money and leverage it with other donors."

Just north of CFSV is the Peninsula Community Foundation (PCF), founded in 1964, which also counts among its corporate clientele prominent technology companies, most notably, Yahoo. "We manage the Yahoo Employees Foundation," says Sterling Speirn, PCF president. This is a foundation funded by employees of the Internet company, "from the top executives down to line workers." He says the Yahoo foundation is "very democratic" in its decision-making, obtaining employee input on where to make grants. Because of that, the grants are very far-reaching, ranging from healthcare to the arts to education, although "you can only apply to Yahoo for a grant if there's a Yahoo employee involved with your organization," Speirn notes. PCF also advises other companies, including Applied Materials and Handspring, on their corporate giving funds. Yahoo employees give through payroll deductions and also donate stock; Applied Materials and Handspring fund their contributions in stock. Stock donations are a common practice in Silicon Valley and other entrepreneurial strongholds, but one that resulted in a heavy drop in the value of donations to many organizations during the current economic downturn. Speirn says gifts to PCF in 2002 dropped back to their 1998 level.

Speirn believes that, in difficult times, corporations should fund nonprofits with proven results. "If you're thoughtful about looking for best practices, you can find the best models. In the nonprofit world, everybody wants to fund you if you've got a clever, creative idea. But when you're 4 to 5 years old and have consistently produced results, nobody's interested." Speirn says it's important to fund sustainability as well as innovation. "The approach, when you find a great nonprofit, should be to buy and hold. You need a long-term horizon." Community foundations can help with that. "We give you instant access to expertise and deal flow," by which he means grant proposals. (Foundation heads in Silicon Valley tend to slip into venture capital-speak, talking about investments and deal flow. Indeed, both CFSV and PCF operate venture philanthropy funds for wealthy individuals.) One of the roles of community foundations "is to be a coach and mentor to local corporate leaders" in determining what to do with their philanthropic dollars, Speirn adds. It's more efficient to give through a community foundation because then "you don't have to build up your knowledge base. It's already here."

The Northern Virginia Technology Council (NVTC) Foundation, based in Herndon, Virginia, focuses on technology projects for its 1,500 member companies, ranging from Time Warner to much smaller entities. About 60 percent of members have 10 employees or fewer. "Although many of the member companies wanted to do something [philanthropically], their reluctance was that they had to put a lot of due diligence and research into creating the project," says Tim Nurvala, president of the foundation. "We provided that. We were the bridge between where many of our companies were and where they wanted to be on community involvement." One major initiative is the Computer Clubhouses. There are now three locations in low-income areas that serve children and adults by providing computers and Internet access. Companies donate various equipment and the foundation brings in system integrators "to put it all together," says Nurvala. The Clubhouses also create ample opportunities for employee involvement, although the foundation first will do a background check on those who want to participate. "Whenever you're working with children, you have to do that," he notes. Once vetted, employees can mentor kids by helping them with homework or talking about a career path. "We show companies how they can get employees involved, giving them an opportunity to interact with each other in a nonbusiness environment," Nurvala says.

The NVTC foundation, which takes both cash and stock contributions, also sponsors educational scholarships, allows local children with serious illnesses to "make a technology wish" and matches that up with company donations, mentors students and senior citizens in use of technology, and sponsors a regional robotics tournaments for students. "We keep the drumbeat on all our member companies to encourage them to give something back," says Nurvala. "We also encourage them to explore how they can give back on their own." Once a year, in partnership with the Washington (D.C.) Regional Association of Grantmakers, NTVC offers a half-day forum for companies that are thinking of starting their own foundation. "AOL doesn't need my help," he says, "but small 10-member firms do." NTVC offers these firms the ability to pool their funding or to get help in doing their own philanthropy. "We find that because we're doing a lot of the structural work, we enable even very small firms to participate," Nurvala notes. "Most of them want to participate. The entrepreneurs don't want their companies to be just about making money."

Entrepreneurs Foundations

Entrepreneurs foundations are very similar to community foundations, except that they specialize in new companies and/or entrepreneurs. In fact, entrepreneurs foundations are often operated by community foundations, such as the Triangle Entrepreneurs Partnership in Research Triangle Park, North Carolina, part of the Triangle Community Foundation. "Working with a community foundation can be beneficial—particularly to entrepreneurial companies," says Shannon St. John, president of the Triangle Community Foundation. "We become the professional philanthropic advisor and staff for the donor or company. The entrepreneurs can define the agenda and the goals and rely on us to help them find the most effective ways of carrying out those goals." She notes that "the marginal cost of sharing our knowledge with them is very small. The marginal cost of building their own organization is substantial." With entrepreneurial companies, she says, the emphasis is on developing a product and building the company. "They don't want to try to build that learning curve with philanthropy."

Triangle Community Foundation manages about three dozen corporate funds; in the Entrepreneurs' Partnership there are 72 heads of companies. (Triangle also operates a Venture Fund that accepts prepublic equity from entrepreneurs, which it turns into cash when the entrepreneur's company has its initial public offering, or IPO.) The Entrepreneurs Partnership requires a gift of $5,000 to join. "The partnership is a club to learn about philanthropy and network with others, but not to give by committee," St. John explains. The members are people "who don't want to give by committee. They want to direct their own funds," either on a corporate or family basis. She adds that corporations and entrepreneurs "come to us because they want a professional partner in their philanthropy, but they don't want a professional dictator in their philanthropy. " She says the range of involvement is threefold: At the top level, Triangle will work with the company/entrepreneur to define goals, then select nonprofits that meet those goals and make donations; at the second level, companies will select from Triangle's list of recommendations for the donations; at the third level, Triangle merely acts as a fund administrator, writing a check to the designated recipients. "We don't encourage that, because donors are not getting the value added of our expertise in screening recipients," St. John says.

The Entrepreneurs Foundation (EF) in San Jose started up in 1998, with the intent of taking advantage of the many "liquidity events"—initial public stock offerings—in Silicon Valley. Companies donate a prescribed amount of prepublic stock and, in turn, get assistance in structuring their philanthropy. When the company actually goes public, half of the donated stock is earmarked for a philanthropic fund or foundation and the other half goes to EF's community relation services, according to Executive Director Diane Solinger. "For all those companies that don't have Marc Benioff at the helm saying I want to do it myself, we're here for them," she says. Five affiliated Entrepreneurs Foundations have sprung up in the United States, located in Portland, Oregon; Dallas and Austin, Texas; Atlanta, Georgia; and Boston, Massachusetts; and one international affiliate has now started in Tel Aviv, Israel. "They're all working with emerging companies based on the stock model we established," Solinger says.

EF offers two levels of assistance. The first is called the Impact Program and requires a donation of $50,000 worth of stock (this is prepublic, so it will be worth considerably more when the company reaches liquidity). "That's the get-your-feet-wet program," Solinger says, designed for very young companies that want to give something back through a community involvement program. EF will provide them with three or four volunteer events a year in which they can join. For a $75,000 stock donation, companies join the Leadership Program. At this level, EF customizes its work. "We will do an employee survey and try to match corporate interests," she says. For example, EF will structure volunteer projects and group activities for team-building, coordinate employee giving, and facilitate marketing wrapped around these efforts.

Although EF is not a venture philanthropy fund, it does work closely with the venture capital (VC) investment community to reach out to company CEOs and other executives. Solinger says she tries to find a VC investor who sits on the company's board and "believes the community is a stakeholder and that philanthropy is a component of a good company." VCs or entrepreneurs who have "made it" and now sit on other companies' boards provide the entrée for EF, she says. Solinger believes that philanthropy, at an early stage, can help create a strong corporate culture. "Employees are more dedicated because you have a sense of team, a greater sense of satisfaction," she says. "What's keeping people together is culture; they like working at a place where there's a sense that it's about something greater than just money." Many venture capitalists understand the importance of having that component. "We don't ask them to compel philanthropy," Solinger notes. "We ask them to support the executives if they want to do philanthropy." Since late 2000, Solinger has developed a volunteer network of more than 70 venture capitalists and secured more than 30 equity contributions from companies. In 2002, she says, 12 companies donated at the $50,000 or $75,000 level, mostly the latter, "because they want to make more of an impact." Her goal in 2003 was to get 20 new companies to sign on; as of early December, 18 had joined and EF was working on two more.

However, in the economic downturn of the early 2000s, which struck Silicon Valley particularly hard, EF had to find other sources of funding to tide it over until the stock market recovered and IPOs became more common. Solinger says EF does receive direct cash grants from both individuals and companies. And, in 2003, it was also advising four companies that had gone public and were getting ready to set up their own grant-making foundations or give to a community foundation. Once companies have monies to devote to philanthropy, EF can provide a donor-advised fund that "essentially trains people in corporate grant-making," she says. "We want to continue to support organizations we've been partnering with by matching gifts to where employees are volunteering." So the work that EF does initially, in building up employee volunteerism, can be enriched with grants to the nonprofits once the company is liquid. EF partners with about 60 community organizations.

Solinger says that small entrepreneurial companies and nonprofits have more in common than they may realize. "Both of them are stretched for resources and never have enough to get the job done," she says. At the same time, EF can act as a bridge to smooth over cultural differences. For instance, "about 80 percent of the employees we're reaching have not volunteered in the community before or are foreign born and are unfamiliar with philanthropy," Solinger notes. "We want to make sure they have positive experiences, that they actually understand why they're doing it." The benefits for the nonprofits, even if they don't get immediate grants, are utilizing the skills of employee volunteers and establishing a relationship with a company that could be big one day.

Other Intermediaries

In many metropolitan areas, corporations and other philanthropists have access to organizations that promote effective grant-making. These are essentially a "foundation of foundations," which bring together donors and nonprofits in an effort to improve communication and promote best practices. Their membership consists of grant-making organizations, including corporate, community, and private foundations, with dues assessed based on total annual grants awarded. A prime example is the Northern California Grantmakers (NCG) in San Francisco, which consists of more than 140 grantmaking organizations in the Bay Area that, together, donate more than $1 billion annually. Building on an initiative started in 1965 to exchange ideas, improve cooperation among foundations, and increase its knowledge of community problems, NCG is focused on two areas: enhancing the effectiveness of philanthropy and strengthening the ties between philanthropy and its stakeholders in nonprofit organizations, government, business, media, academia, and the public at large. Corporate programs represent about 20 percent of NCG's membership, according to Judy Berger, NCG's senior program executive.

NCG offers programs and workshops to enable members to develop grant-making skills and become acquainted with current practices on issues such as accountability, relationships with grantees, responsiveness to changing demographics and community needs, new regulations, and emerging trends. "What we do at NCG is provide educational programs in two general areas—content topics, like the latest in education and the arts, and sector-specific opportunities," Berger explains. For example, in 2003, it sponsored a workshop on the latest regulations and trends in philanthropy by banks and another on measuring philanthropic outcomes (see next chapter). NCG also helps to facilitate "affinity groups" within its membership, such as sponsoring a Corporate Community Relations Council and a Corporate Contributors roundtable. NCG also sponsors four collaborative funds that bring various donors together—the AIDS Partnership California, Arts Loan Fund, Emergency Fund, and Summer Youth Project.

Berger sees the role of corporate philanthropy as being an active, positive player in communities. "It's a way for businesses to both give back and invest," she says. "Giving back is the altruistic part; investment is the smart-business part." That epitomizes the ongoing debate in corporate philanthropy: "Do you do it because it's the right thing to do, or because it smart?" Berger's smart response: It's both. "It's appropriate for businesses to support their communities. There is, if not a short-term payback, a long-term payback." She praises corporations that continue to "step up to the plate" even in difficult economic times, singling out Wells Fargo as one that has increased its giving (see Chapter 7). "If you're doing well, you have more to give—but so many are not doing well that it puts a tremendous burden on those who are," she says. Berger is candid in acknowledging that "maximizing the PR benefit of philanthropy is of real interest to our members." Corporations want to mix altruism with the advancement of their business strategy. "It's an approach that raises questions but provides windows of opportunity for enhancing the company's ability to make a positive difference," she says. "When you're taking shareholder dollars, or dollars that might go into hiring or reducing the price of products, and giving it to charities, you need to let people know what you're doing and why. The more altruism is seen as part of your strategy, the better it works to your advantage."

Two national organizations, both based in Washington, serve as umbrella groups for regional grantmakers. They are the Grantmakers for Effective Organizations (GEO) and the Forum of Regional Associations of Grantmakers. GEO, which absorbed the similar Grantmakers Evaluation

Network in late 2002, sponsors conferences, publications, and research devoted to "learning and encouraging dialogue among funders committed to building strong and effective nonprofit organizations." The Forum represents 29 regional associations of grant-makers (such as NCG) that encompass more than 4,000 grant-making organizations. The Forum, which cosponsors an annual conference with GEO, seeks to connect grant-makers with intermediaries and other advisors, as well as with each other, in an effort to facilitate collaboration, support, and professional development. The two are also good sources of information about grant-making intermediaries in different regions. GEO Executive Director Kathleen Enright says that corporations, no matter how good they are in meeting their business goals, have much to learn when it comes to philanthropy. "They need to pair up with collegial philanthropy organizations who have been doing this for years," she says. "For awhile there was this posture that we [in business] know how to fix you [nonprofits]. You need to run like a business." After the scandals at Enron and other companies, that message doesn't play so well, she says, advising corporations that they need to "understand your audience and be humble about your own knowledge."

A Helping Hand

Intermediary organizations exist in virtually all areas of the country. Most nonprofits will know about them and can direct companies to them if they're not readily apparent. For companies new to philanthropy, or even for larger companies that want to take a fresh look at what they're doing in the community, intermediaries can be a valuable partner. The relationship, as demonstrated in the examples cited here, does not have to be a long-term one. It can be structured to allow the corporate philanthropic organization to build up a knowledge base while still doing effective giving. One of the toughest jobs in philanthropy is saying no. Indeed, a good philanthropic program probably winds up saying no more than yes because, as word spreads, it's going to get more and more grant requests. Says NTVC's Nurvala: "Companies may make the mistake of trying to do too much and overextending, then not doing the homework on the nonprofits." For example, a company will contribute to a day-care center down the street on the recommendation of an employee who uses it without "realizing the paperwork, time, and effort involved."

Managing contributions, Nurvala sums up, "does become a huge part of somebody's job." So, if you don't want to assign someone internally, make sure you have an external partner up to the task.

An intermediary can help a corporation establish its goals, define what types of grant requests it will take, sift through those requests, and conduct "due diligence" on the nonprofits. Once a company establishes its philanthropy, it can refine the relationship, taking on more responsibility internally if it so desires. The most important issues in dealing with an intermediary include communicating goals and parameters, clearly defining each entity's role, and making sure that the intermediary is itself a sustainable enterprise. After that, it's up to the company as to how much, or how little, it wants to rely on an intermediary.

The Different Ways to Give

Community foundations and entrepreneur funds offer a variety of services to corporate givers. Among the options are:

▶ **Pooled fund:** Companies pool donations into a larger fund, run by the foundation that selects the nonprofit recipients based on input from the participating contributors. Can be a good first step for smaller companies just getting started in philanthropy.

▶ **Corporate-advised fund:** Often referred to interchangeably with a donor-advised fund (aimed at individuals), these specifically tailored funds help companies design a corporate giving program and establish employee volunteerism. Can be used as an interim step toward running your own program.

▶ **Venture philanthropy fund:** Aimed at either individual entrepreneurs or corporations, these funds act like venture capitalists in "investing" contributions in a variety of nonprofits. They attempt to apply the rules of venture capital investing to nonprofits by designating a series of benchmarks. Can be useful for companies that want to donate prepublic stock rather than cash.

Measuring Philanthropy

O ne disconnect that often flares up between the corporate and nonprofit worlds concerns how to measure the impact of philanthropic programs. Corporations, whether public or private, devote a lot of energy to tracking results with profit-and-loss statements, cash flow, inventory, profit, revenue, product sales, and so on. The accounting scandals at companies such as Enron and WorldCom demonstrate that companies can subvert these measures, but, still, the improper practices eventually come to light. There are oversight bodies—the Financial Accounting Standards Board and the Securities and Exchange Commission—whose job is to make sure that companies provide an agreed-upon set of measurements as part of their public statements. (Private companies are exempt from disclosure, of course, but internally they use very similar measures.) Most reasonably knowledgeable people who pick up a corporate income statement or balance sheet can recognize the important features such as net income, earnings per share, liabilities versus equity, and so forth, and apply that to determining how successful or unsuccessful the company is.

The same is not true of the nonprofit world. To be sure, 501(c)(3) organizations—the Internal Revenue Service's designation for a nonprofit charity—and foundations have to file tax information about their asset base and the amount disbursed every year to the community, but these statements give you no idea of how effectively that money has been used. For example, Nonprofit X could be spending millions on helping the homeless, but does that translate into fewer people on the street and more people with jobs and stable housing, or does it merely create a culture of dependency? And who determines the measures of success? The donor or the recipient? For corporations, the problem is compounded by the fact that not only do they want their philanthropy to be devoted to "impactful" programs, but they'd also like to know if doing philanthropy benefits them internally—such as in attracting or retaining employees, generating good public relations, or improving their standing in the eyes of shareholders. "When people talk about measuring impact, they mean all sorts of different things," says Dinah Waldsmith, senior manager at Business for Social Responsibility, a nonprofit consultant. "Impact is really hard to measure," she adds. "When people say they're measuring impact, what they're usually satisfied with is quantifying that which is quantifiable, using numbers wrapped around anecdotes." For example, a giving program donating to a homeless shelter looks at number of people served.

Then there's the time element. Corporations, obviously, are conditioned to producing quarterly and annual statements. Today, thanks to technology, they can track many indicators on a daily or even hourly basis, such as inventory inflows and outflows, hits to a Website, or calls to an 800 number. With philanthropy, it's difficult to produce precise periodic measurements, and, even if you do, they can be meaningless. A homeless shelter, no doubt, can tell you how many meals it serves each day to how many people. But if it's serving fewer meals, does that mean the number of homeless is decreasing or the food is lousy? "Philanthropy requires patience—measuring things over long periods of time," says Waldsmith. She singles out IBM as one company that understands this. In its Reinventing Education program, Big Blue recognized that measures of success had to be long term. Over the years, "you can see how children's education improved," she says, based on measures such as graduation rates and test scores, but the effect will be gradual and cumulative, not immediate.

"Everyone's wrestling with how to measure [philanthropy] in a way that is meaningful and practical," Waldsmith adds, but cautions that measurement cannot be homogenous, as it is in the corporate world. "You have to look at the system in which the nonprofit exists, what the operating constraints are." There are significant differences, she notes, between, say, a performing arts center, an educational tutoring program, and a homeless shelter. So measures of impact will have to be different. In this chapter, we examine some of the more credible efforts to determine the value of philanthropy, with special thanks to two reports that we will use extensively: "Philanthropy Measures Up," from the World Economic Forum, and "Measurement Demystified: Determining the Value of Corporate Community Involvement," by the Center for Corporate Citizenship at Boston College.

Differing Approaches

Numerous organizations have developed methods to assess philanthropic effectiveness, some looking at the grantees and some at the grant-makers. Three that have achieved recognition are the Roberts Enterprise Development Fund (REDF), which uses an internally developed Social Return on Investment (SROI) to consider its own grantees; New Profit, Inc., which uses a Balanced Scorecard to measure individual grantees as well as its overall portfolio; and the Center for Effective Philanthropy, which surveys grantees of foundations on their opinions about the foundation's performance.

Founded in 1997 in San Francisco, with funding from leveraged buyout specialist George Roberts (of Kohlberg Kravis Roberts & Co.), REDF has a mission to help homeless and low-income individuals move out of poverty by partnering with Bay Area nonprofits to create jobs and training opportunities in social-purpose enterprises. In doing so, it has created a very specific and rather complex metric to determine how effectively nonprofits are accomplishing this. First, the SROI calculates an economic value based on the total cash the social-purpose enterprise is expected to generate if the business continues indefinitely. That value is then compared to total investment (that is, donations) in the enterprise to come up with an enterprise index, showing how much financial value is created per dollar invested. Second, SROI calculates a social-purpose value, which it defines as the dollar amount of the public-cost savings and increased tax revenue generated by individuals while they're employed by the enterprise. This value is compared to total investment, creating a social-purpose index that shows how much social value is generated per dollar invested. Finally, the SROI combines these two values to create a blended index that measures how much an investment is returning.

The World Economic Forum calls the SROI "the best known, best documented, most transparent system we have seen for measuring the impact of one's grantees on society."[1] However, its applicability is limited to social enterprises that have financial as well as social goals. Melinda Tuan, REDF's managing director and cofounder, says George Roberts "wanted his philanthropy to go into something that made sense to him," so the fund began surveying the social-enterprise businesses on what they were accomplishing in the lives of their employees. For example, were they using fewer services such as food stamps and welfare? Eventually, this developed into the SROI. The process of calculating SROI "is intensive," she acknowledges. REDF budgets $150,000 "just to do the surveys" of employees and social enterprises and has a consulting firm that figures out all of the data. "It's obviously not appropriate to use this [SROI] if you're giving a $10,000 grant," Tuan says. "If you could coordinate with other funders to do this, that would be great." She believes that the SROI could be used as a basis to measure other types of philanthropy, but it will take work. One of the most important aspects of SROI, she believes, is "that we came up with a figure based on taxpayer dollars saved. Very few nonprofits have as their goal saving taxpayer dollars."

New Profit is a venture philanthropy fund in Cambridge, Massachusetts, that raises money from wealthy individuals, foundations, and corporations to invest in "social entrepreneurs who are ready to grow," according to Kelly Fitzsimmons, managing partner and cofounder. Its Balanced Scorecard is a performance measurement and management tool used to document the results of a social entrepreneurial strategy, including looking at the objectives (what the strategy is trying to achieve), measures (how success is measured), and goals (the level of performance necessary to be successful). New Profit uses the scorecard to measure each venture in which it invests, as well as its own overall portfolio performance. "We link our investees' performance to our own and give reports to our investors each quarter," she says. "The scorecard looks at the types of measures that tell you what's going on—process and outputs." Some of those measures include the compound annual growth rate by revenue and by number of lives touched. There are also quality indicators such as, for example, gains in children's reading scores related to a literacy program. Finally, New Profit figures out how much leverage an invested dollar creates in cash and services by the nonprofit. "We want our portfolio companies to hit their benchmarks. They've got to be raising money on their own—grants, earned income, individual contributions, contracts," Fitzsimmons emphasizes.

She believes that the Balanced Scorecard has wider applicability than REDF's SROI, although "we would encourage organizations doing job skills training to use [the latter]," says Fitzsimmons. Unlike SROI, which has not been tried much in corporate philanthropy, the Balanced Scorecard comes out of the for-profit world and is used by some corporate foundations, including the NASDAQ Foundation, she says. Fitzsimmons says the Balanced Scorecard is sensitive to the differences between for-profit and nonprofit measures. "We spent a lot of time adapting the business and for-profit stuff for applications in the nonprofit sector," she says. "We want to put in place interim measures that show us we're on track for longer term." For example, Citizen Schools, one of New Profit's grantees, does direct interventions with at-risk middle school students. Long-term measures include improvement in grades, improved scores on the state standardized exams, and higher rates of college enrollment. "All three of those things clearly don't lend themselves to a quarterly measurement," Fitzsimmons acknowledges. But there are learning assessment tools that "we can use to track progress, like writing skills of these students, while we're waiting for longer-term metrics." She says New Profit worked with Citizen schools to "mutually determine the measures." She adds, "We don't just rely on our own assumptions. We bring in third-party experts to punch holes in the assumptions or strengthen them."

The Center for Effective Philanthropy, also in Cambridge, was founded by business gurus Michael Porter and Mark Kramer. Unlike the other two methods described previously, which hone in on the performance of grantees, the Center's grantee perception report looks at how well foundations themselves are doing in meeting the needs of recipients. The report focuses on four areas: achieving impact, including program and grant objectives; setting the strategy, including focus areas, establishing achievable goals, and choosing an approach; managing operations, including the grantee selection process and responsiveness; and optimizing governance, including accountability, stewardship, and active engagement. The Center did a preliminary study of grantee perceptions related to 23 foundations and, in 2003, was expanding that to the 100 largest foundations in the United States. The idea was to make comparative and aggregate data available, so that each participating foundation could assess its own performance versus that of its peers. Says Kramer: "We are trying to get at how the foundations select grantees and interact with them. Most of the others [measurement efforts] are looking at what the grantee did with the money." In 2003, he says, the center mailed surveys to 11,000 grantees that had received donations from major foundations and received 6,000 responses, covering 58 of the largest foundations. "We asked about a wide range of specifics, from how long it takes to get a grant approved to the fairness in getting a grant to the estimate of impact," Kramer says. Other questions included how well the foundation understands the field where it's making grants. At first, the survey was used with private foundations, but "in the next year or two, we will be offering this as a tool to corporate foundations."

The SROI in Action

Here's a real-life example of how the Social Return on Investment (SROI), developed by the Roberts Enterprise Development Fund, works. Einstein's Café in San Francisco, operated by Youth Industry, provides transitional and permanent jobs and training to homeless youth. In 1999, its target number of employees was 35, all from 14 to 24 years old. The SROI calculated that Einstein's is saving society $12,389 in social service costs and public assistance per target employee. The net financial improvement to the target employee is $5,174 annually. This translates to a social-purpose value of about $7 million and a social index of return greater than 27 times what was invested. Einstein's Café became profitable less than three years after opening, with sales of $415,404 in 1999 and projected sales of $490,177 in 2000. Based on investment to date (at the time) of $255,671, the SROI is $31.47 generated in blended value (financial and social purpose) for every dollar invested.

Source: Roberts Enterprise Development Fund

Gauging Corporate Impact

In 2003, the World Economic Forum report found only one system specifically focused on measuring the impact of corporate philanthropy on the corporation itself, a joint project offered by Walker Information and the Council on Foundations (for more information, visit *www.measuringphilanthropy.com*). Walker Info is a private, for-profit company based in Indianapolis that specializes in using information-based products and measurement sciences to access, discover, and apply new knowledge and insight. In 2000, Walker Info did a preliminary survey for the Council on Foundations about measuring the business value of corporate philanthropy. That evolved into a survey-based measurement tool, the Corporate Philanthropy Index (CPI), intended to demonstrate the link between the perceptions of stakeholders (including employees, shareholders, customers, and influencers such as the media) and their willingness to embrace corporate philanthropy. First, the CPI asks survey participants to rate companies' philanthropic activity, from 1 (strongly disagree) to 5 (strongly agree), in three areas: whether company X does its fair share to help the community; if it contributes time, volunteers, money, and sponsorships to nonprofit causes; and if it seems to care about helping the community. Stakeholders also respond to queries about their attitude toward the company, including feelings about its reputation and public image, and about their behavior, whether they're likely to continue to work for or with the company, recommend the company to others, and so forth.

Walker Info Chairman Frank Walker, now semi-retired, says his mother founded the company in 1939 and his son is the third generation to run it. For him, "measuring ethical culture has become a passion," as he leads the company's CPI efforts. "I was raised to give back," he says, but with so many companies claiming to be socially responsible, "how do you differentiate?" In the 1990s Walker Info did a study to see what the public thought of the term "social responsibility." Respondents identified things such as financial stability, support for communities, concern for employees, protection of the environment, and ethical business practices. Walker then approached the Council on Foundations about developing a joint product, which resulted in the CPI. However, he concedes that using such a tool has yet to win many adherents. The survey is expensive and resource-intensive, and "I would be less than candid if I said people were knocking down the door to use it," Walker says. None of the companies interviewed for this book were utilizing the Walker survey, although a few were asking employees what they thought about philanthropy and its importance as a retention factor.

The CPI in Action

A joint project of Walker Information and the Council on Foundations, the Corporate Philanthropy Index (CPI) rates companies' philanthropic activity in three areas:

1. Compared to other companies, X does its fair share to help the community and society.

2. Overall, X is the kind of company that helps the community and society by contributing things such as time, volunteers, money, and sponsorships of nonprofit events and causes.

3. X really seems to care about giving and making contributions to help the community and society.

Each item is measured on a five-point scale, from 1 (strongly disagree) to 5 (strongly agree). Companies testing multiple groups can either average scores across groups or report separate figures for each individual group.

Another goal of the project is to demonstrate a link between CPI ratings and outcomes. To achieve this, stakeholders, such as employees, are asked to rate the company on several "attitude" and "behavioral intention" factors.

"Attitude" factors include:

▸ Overall reputation is excellent.

▸ Overall image is positive.

▸ X is a good corporate citizen.

- ▸ X is admired for its good deeds.

- ▸ Generosity differentiates the company.

- ▸ I feel a sense of goodwill toward the company.

- ▸ I'll give it the benefit of doubt if there's negative publicity.

"Behavioral intention" factors include:

- ▸ I'm likely to continue with the company.

- ▸ I'm likely to recommend company offerings.

- ▸ I would choose the company again.

- ▸ I'm likely to switch for a better financial deal.

The research showed a strong link between high CPI ratings and positive attitudes and behavioral intentions toward the company

Source: *Philanthropy Measures Up* by the World Economic Forum

Walker continues to believe that it's important for companies to get stakeholder opinions about their philanthropic endeavors. "Financials are not a good predictor of [the company's] future," he contends. "We think stakeholders' attitudes predict the future. Our model suggests that if we can figure out what is driving the impressions and attitudes, we can predict behavior." For instance, Walker surveys have shown a close link between high CPI ratings and positive attitudes and behavioral intentions toward the company. Employees were more likely to remain with a company that they thought was giving back to the community. Customers were more likely to recommend the company to others. Besides, he adds, as far as corporate philanthropy, "we're the only game in town."

That's not quite true. Some corporations, including IBM and Hewlett-Packard, have turned to academia to help them measure philanthropy.

IBM, along with six other North American companies, was a "best-practice partner" in the Center for Corporate Citizenship at Boston College's study of corporate philanthropy. HP has engaged a faculty member from Stanford University to assist in assessing its Digital Village initiative. Still other corporations have enlisted outside consultants. But what an earlier study by the Boston College Center concluded is that "almost universally, corporations were struggling with how to determine the impact of their (community involvement) programs in systematic and comprehensive ways." This fits with what we found in researching this book: most of the corporate philanthropic organizations we interviewed believed that measurement was important, but almost none thought that what they were doing was adequate. Starbucks was fairly typical. Externally, it sets goals jointly with the nonprofits it funds. "We do the traditional evaluations required of foundation grants," says Lauren Moore, director of the Starbucks Foundation. At the beginning, "we may do a memo of understanding on what each side will provide. Then we ask for an end-of-grant report from the organization back to us." Internally, she says, one of her jobs "is trying to make sure people know these programs exist." Because Starbucks is a retail organization with considerable turnover, "it's a constant challenge to communicate what we're doing." In their exit interviews, "many people say these programs are wonderful; I wish I'd known about them before," she adds. On the other hand, those employees familiar with the philanthropic efforts say that's one of the qualities that make Starbucks an attractive place to work.

It's probably no surprise that the companies spending the biggest bucks on major, multiyear philanthropic initiatives are most determined to measure their impact. Let's go back to IBM and HP with, respectively, Reinventing Education and Digital Village. In Chapter 10, we already described RE's impact externally, with improvements in student test scores and teacher professional development at school districts that received the grants. But IBM also trumpets the internal gains that resulted from its $75-million investment. Says Stan Litow, president of the IBM Foundation: "We look at the intellectual capital [we've gained as a result], including the number of patents. These projects also offer training opportunities for staff—they pick up new skills." He adds that IBM studies the impact of community service on attracting and retaining employees. "It's definitely a positive," Litow says. Finally, IBM looks at press clippings. In the United States, about 25 percent of the media coverage of IBM concerns various community relations topics. "Community service tends to be the largest single topic" that the press writes about in relation to Big Blue, according to Litow.

In a recent presentation to a conference sponsored by the Northern California Grantmakers titled "Measuring Up: Assessing the Value and Impact of Corporate Philanthropy," Janet Rocco, IBM's Northwest region manager of corporate community relations, reviewed some of the company's gains from RE. These included two new products developed as a result of working with schools (speech recognition software that's being marketed by an outside company and a data warehousing application), six patents, and various corporate citizenship awards. It received the 2002 Good Corporate Citizen award from the Points of Light Foundation; the 2000 and 2002 award for Most Ethical Corporation from Business Ethics; and the 2002 Leaders for Change award from the Council for Aid to Education. And, although this is harder to document, Rocco believes the IBM culture is strengthened by community service. "The executives and employees feel like it's part of their job to follow the drummer of corporate philanthropy. They don't question whether they have to do this," she says.

The Boston College Center, which did an assessment of IBM's programs as part of its study, concludes that the company's community relations activities strive to underscore the role of technology as a tool to address societal issues, demonstrate IBM's reputation as a solid solutions provider, and enhance IBM's relationship with customers and employees. "A key focus…is developing new products and services that address social needs," the report states. "Many of these products and services are then marketed to the company's business partners and customers.…The 'win-win' in this collaboration is twofold. IBM grantees benefit from the newly developed technology solutions that are being created to address their needs. IBM, in turn, can utilize the grantees as testing sites for these new technology solutions, which IBM can then refine and bring to scale for its commercial market. Many of IBM's community partners have even become loyal customers for IBM's business."[2]

David M. Fetterman, director of the Policy Analysis and Evaluation Program at Stanford's School of Education, is working with each of HP's three U.S. Digital Villages—in East Palo Alto, the Indian tribal lands in San Diego County, and Baltimore—to implement his "empowerment evaluation" processes and tools. HP, Fetterman, and leaders of the three "villages" jointly decide the metrics to be used, and then the Digital Villages track and report their own progress on such measures as job development, computer use in the schools, formation of technology centers, and the like. In this way, Fetterman says, even after the formal grant period concludes (as it has with East Palo Alto), the community still has the tools to continue refining the progress. "Evaluation helps them develop a clear logic for what they're doing and evaluate those strategies on an ongoing basis and change them in real time," says Fetterman. It's not very easy to impose traditional measurement on the Digital Villages, he notes. "This approach builds individual local capacity, rather than just getting the job done and leaving nothing behind, which is the typical approach. This is focused on sustainability."

In working directly with the villages, Fetterman describes himself as a coach and facilitator, helping people understand "what they want to accomplish, how to accomplish it, and how to evaluate it." The first thing he does is hold a "where are we now?" workshop devoted to prioritizing the key activities. Then each of those is assessed on a 1 to 10 scale, 1 being *pathetic*, in Fetterman's words, and 10 *perfect*. "They all go through three steps: establish the mission, take stock of where they are, and plan for the future," he says. He videotapes this initial workshop and then, in three months, "we go back and say let's see where we are now; put the video on and say here's what we committed to." This process repeats itself as the multiyear-grant period unfolds. "The idea of empowerment evaluation is that you're internalizing it," he says. Fetterman recalls working with the Indian tribal nations, a process that helped them realize all that they had accomplished with the Digital Village. "They know now that, given the opportunity, they can do things like create a wireless system and operate it." Tribal members have also gone through the Cisco Network Academy training. "It's not about technology per se, but the knowledge gains they make in terms of using it—jobs, security, education," says Fetterman. "Technology is intriguing, but what people are doing with it to change their lives is even more intriguing."

Fetterman praises HP's approach to the Digital Villages as being that of equal partner, not dictator. In one case in Baltimore, "the group wasn't ready to show HP where they were yet, so they uninvited [HP] to a status report meeting," he says. With most corporate philanthropists, "that would be shooting yourself in the head. HP, to their credit, said we understand and we'll wait until you pull it together." Fetterman met with the community leadership group alone, facilitated a discussion, and helped them prepare a status report. "In my experience, no one feels comfortable enough to uninvite a funder," he says, "but they wanted to do it right and trusted HP to let them." Too often, if philanthropic projects appear to be lagging, the corporate funder will step in and prod them to speed up. "Many companies become control freaks," he says. "They don't have enough trust to let go, let [community leaders] make their own mistakes." These companies may do a "phenomenal job" of running a philanthropic project, but when they go, "they won't leave these people with the skills to do it themselves." With the Digital Villages, "people who got the opportunity to develop these programs became more professional, and that will prepare them for markets outside they wouldn't have had a chance at before."

HP's evaluation process builds in a corrective feedback mechanism that also benefits the company, Fetterman adds. "They want to know, 'Are people using this stuff [their technology]?' and what they could do better." Not only that, the lessons from the Digital Villages can be applied both in HP's other philanthropic efforts and to its commercial ones. "When I first started working with HP, I asked them about their agenda," he recalls. "They said they wanted to make sure that the technology was useful to people. Of course they also wanted to sell more technology down the road."

Debra Dunn, HP's senior vice president of corporate affairs, acknowledges that measurement of a project such as Digital Village is very complicated. With other HP philanthropy, it's a little easier. For example, with educational programs, "we can track literacy and employment levels to see if it's made a difference. We can look at things like test scores." She adds that "we can't claim success in terms of the social value we contribute if we can't demonstrate impact in some key indicators, but these are often hard to measure and it takes resources to do it right." Echoing Fetterman, she points out that in all the philanthropic work that HP does, "we try to create a community and enable it to become a learning sharing community." As for the impact of philanthropy on HP itself, "we're beginning to do brand measurement in this whole area of global citizenship," says Dunn, asking questions of opinion leaders about their perception of HP. In employee surveys, "we ask about philanthropy." HP also publishes a monthly internal newsletter called *Global Citizenship*, which employees can opt out of, although "very few say they don't want it," Dunn reports. "People like to know they work for a company that does stuff like this. There's pressure from many stakeholders, including share owners, around good corporate citizenship."

It's All About Teamwork

Four conclusions about measuring the impact of philanthropy emerge from the research that went into this chapter. The first: *It's not there yet.* That is, there is no universal set of indicators such as a corporate income statement that every nonprofit or foundation can produce annually, and there probably never will be, outside of the tax statements required by the IRS, because community needs are too complex to be neatly pigeonholed. The second: *Any metrics that are adopted must be flexible and customized.* They have to be designed in connection with the particular project at hand, and then followed and refined as the project continues. This also applies to the corporation's efforts to measure impact internally. Anecdotal reports from employees about their involvement in community service do carry weight, especially if they're communicated effectively to others. The third: *Both short-term and long-term metrics must be considered.* Sure, nonprofits are correct when they state that many of their missions—getting homeless off the street, improving education, providing job training to low-income communities—don't lend themselves to quick fixes. But some measures can be employed fairly swiftly, such as number of people in job training. Others will take longer, such as decreases in the unemployment level of a particular area. Finally and perhaps most importantly: *Whatever measures are adopted must be a matter of teamwork between the corporate donor and the grantee.* Simply imposing businesslike benchmarks upon nonprofits has created more resentment than progress. Rather, the successful programs, such as Digital Village, stress collaboration and toleration of mistakes. They demand not hard numbers, but designation of core goals and outcomes that can be documented.

As consultant Waldsmith puts it, "I ask companies if they could hold themselves to the same standard they're asking of nonprofits." In addition, if it's a difficult standard, "then help pay for devising the measurement. Don't just make a $10,000 grant that's supposed to have amazing results where you don't have any budget for overhead or metrics." The Boston College Center points out that hard numbers aren't the only valid metric. "Key internal stakeholders don't always demand that the [community involvement (CI)] department produces statistically validated, air-tight dollar figures," the Center says in its study. "Instead, they may simply be asking CI managers to follow the same management process that other departments use—a strategy that clearly explains the purpose of CI and its core goals; an action plan that implements the strategy; and measures that demonstrate whether strategic goals are met."[3]

The same reasoning can be applied to the external goals of grantees. Kramer forecasts that the development of viable metrics can be one of the great contributions of corporate philanthropy. "Corporations understand how sustainable economies work," he says. And they also understand the importance of measuring impact, which is beneficial to nonprofits as well. Demonstrable results can attract other donors. "If you're actually having an impact, it will transform corporate philanthropy," Kramer says. "Now there's a reason—a compelling business reason—to put resources behind this. Then [nonprofits] will be able to count on a much larger and more consistent stream of giving."

14

The Nonprofit Perspective

I t's not easy being a nonprofit these days. With a struggling economy, nonprofits are faced with more demand than ever for their services. But sources of funding are harder to come by, and there's more competition for what's left. That means one of two things is necessary: Either cut back on expenditures or creatively find new sources of funding. The latter might be accomplished by reaching out more effectively to the corporate world, which represents a potential source of grant-making growth for beleaguered nonprofits—if they can figure out how to tap it. The barrier, of course, is the disconnect between the corporate and nonprofit worlds that we've alluded to in previous chapters. Corporations increasingly want to focus their philanthropy on big-impact projects that make a difference and on charitable giving that matches their business goals. Nonprofits may grumble all they want about conflict of interest and digression from "pure" philanthropy (when there is really no such thing), but the simple fact remains that corporations have money and other valuable resources. To get a piece of those, you have to play the game according to the rules the corporations set up. This is not to say that corporations shouldn't heed the pleas of nonprofits—some of which we will offer here—for deeper understanding, more sophisticated approaches, and better communication. Indeed, one important goal of this book is to encourage "best practices" by corporate philanthropists, which includes doing the best possible job of working with their nonprofit partners.

Common corporate complaints about the nonprofit world revolve around lack of clear priorities, inefficient use of resources, fuzzy accountability, and sheer foot-dragging in getting anything done. Nonprofits counter that corporations are arrogant, pushy, too ready to apply business methods to problems they may not fit, and unwilling to take the time to learn about the issues. There is also a fundamental suspicion that often exists due to the perception of the other side's ultimate goal. Nonprofits view for-profits as purveyors of corporate greed and materialism at all costs, while the corporation perceives the nonprofit as focused on short-term or reactive issues rather than on systemic change that could eliminate the problem completely. This misperception can lead to nonprofits being less than forthright about the real challenges of their programs and corporations forcing funding projects down paths that may not be the best approach.

These are differences that can—and must—be overcome. There is, after all, considerable common ground between the nonprofit and corporate worlds. The challenges that confront nonprofits are not too different from those that confront corporations: You have to be smarter and run leaner, find ways to do more with less, streamline administrative functions, employ technology effectively, and cooperate with partners and sometimes competitors. Both worlds have value to give to one another; it's not just a matter of a handout from corporations to nonprofits. As has been amply demonstrated with the success of partnerships such as that of Timberland and City Year, the learning goes both ways. Timberland provides money and resources, solid backing, and outreach to other funders; City Year brings diversity training, opportunities for employees and executives to bond in community service projects, and good PR. In this chapter, we present the nonprofit view of corporate giving organizations, both the positives and the negatives, in an effort to bring these separate worlds a little closer together.

The Good

Corporate funders can be extremely valuable not just for cash but for their expertise. SeniorNet, a San Francisco-based nonprofit whose mission is to get seniors online, partners with technology companies such as IBM, eBay, and SBC Communications. IBM has not only sponsored 65 learning centers, it also developed a Web browser for people with low vision or motor impairments. All SeniorNet members can download the software from the site (*www.seniornet.org*). Not only that, "half of our 6,000 volunteers at 240 learning centers around the country are IBM retirees," says SeniorNet President Ann Wrixon. Cofounder of eBay, Jeff Skoll, who also has his own private foundation, has been another strong supporter of SeniorNet. A lot of eBay users are seniors, and, in 2000, Skoll approached SeniorNet "out of the blue," Wrixon says. "He said he was very interested in older adults and technology, and wanted to support what SeniorNet was doing." The meeting culminated in "the dream of what you want to hear as a nonprofit," says Wrixon. Skoll told her, "I love your program. We'll give you an unrestricted grant of $1 million." In nonprofit parlance, "unrestricted" means the grant is not tied to a particular project, but can be used for things such as administration and overhead. (SeniorNet gets $200,000 annually, for five years, under the eBay grant.) Wrixon also worked with eBay to improve the offerings for seniors at the eBay University, which trains people to use the auction site. After 9/11, "Jeff came to me, asked if we were having problems, and what more could he do?" This, she sums up, is exactly what nonprofits need from corporate philanthropy: a genuine give-and-take, exchange of ideas, and services and cash that aren't tied merely to a big project the corporation can brag about.

Another nonprofit that's forged good corporate partnerships is San Jose-based Resource Area for Teachers (RAFT), which provides hardware, software, and classes for teachers to learn about technology. Among its partners are Cadence Design Systems and Adobe Systems. Cadence first got involved with RAFT when it awarded the organization a $450,000 grant from its Stars & Strikes event, but Cadence executives, including CEO Ray Bingham, were so impressed with the program they decided to form an ongoing relationship. "They gave us funds to support replication of our program in areas outside of San Jose," says Mary Simon, RAFT's executive director. Cadence also lent the services of its in-house attorney to help RAFT with legal questions related to expansion, and its facilities management team to aid RAFT in finding new locations. "I feel like I could call Cadence with a need and say we're really stuck and they would help," Simon says. Adobe provides not only cash gifts, but instructors for classes in its software. The company pays the instructors, who are either employees or Adobe-certified consultants. Adobe also contracts with RAFT to manage the administration of its in-house "teach the teacher" program. Says Simon, "Adobe pays for the cost of our staff for the program. It is a contract, not a grant." What she likes about both Adobe and Cadence is that "they believe enough in RAFT that they trust us to make choices."

At first, Starbucks was hesitant about teaming with Conservation International to undertake the coffee-growing initiative described in Chapter 8. "They thought we didn't know anything about coffee," says senior vice president of Conservation International, Glenn Prickett. Consequently, the company was cautious in how it structured the relationship. "We've had written agreements at every stage about what we think the outcomes will be," says Prickett. "There was a sense about not being sure about delivering on promises." Gradually, however, trust built up. "It hasn't been an automatic positive; we've both had to work," he says. "Starbucks has bent over backwards to educate these [coffee-growing] cooperatives on what their standards are." One important facet of success has been support inside of Starbucks by Sue Mecklenberg, the vice president for business practices. "In the strongest corporate partnerships you have a champion at a high level who really takes it on and sticks with it," says Prickett. "Starbucks is a great example. We started with Sue and she walked the halls convincing people." He adds that it also helps when the nonprofit can show how the philanthropic cause—in this case environmentally sustainable coffee production—bolsters the partner's business goals. "These corporations don't exist to give their money away. They need value coming back," he says. "If you can find that synergy, it works extremely well. Your corporate partner is more motivated because their business success is bound up with it."

Echoing Prickett is Bob Goodwin, executive director of the Washington-based Points of Light Foundation. "While everyone should be involved, senior management buy-in and leadership is vital to sustain effective philanthropy," he says. In particular, "when the CEO embraces the

efforts, the programs are protected and even grown during bad times."
He also seconds the notion of programs that are in line with business
goals. The 68 individual company winners (as of 2003) of the Points of
Light awards "all have top-level endorsement and leadership," he says.
Typically, winning corporations pick a philanthropic area, such as mentoring,
improving the environment, or stopping teenage violence, and tie in cash
gifts and employee volunteerism. "They also have accountable persons within
their organizations for how this work reinforces their business goals," says
Goodwin.

The Bad

We've seen the good examples. Now how about the bad? Not sur-
prisingly, nonprofits didn't want to volunteer names, but they were eager
to describe practices that don't work well. *Flexibility*, or *lack* of it, came
up a lot in interviews with nonprofits. With a nonprofit, "you're dealing
with a partner who's very different than a normal business partner," says
Conservation International's Prickett. "A nonprofit is not a contractor.
We don't jump when you say 'jump.'" Consequently, corporations "have
got to learn to be very flexible in terms of their expectations of day-to-day
operations." Tim Nurvala, president of the Northern Virginia Technology
Council Foundation, says the frustration that corporations often express with nonprofits comes because the nonprofit community is focused
on the end—that is, the mission—and not the means. "In the business
world, the structure enables you to fulfill the mission," he says, so
processes such as setting up computer networks or creating financial
accounting systems become very important. "These are secondary for the
nonprofit world," he adds. However, members of the business community,
accustomed to its all-important processes and usually uninterested in
funding administrative costs for nonprofits, "complain that they want
everything done for free and it should have been done yesterday."
Prickett adds that both sides must be willing to compromise and be
mindful of the other's sensitivities. "Nonprofits are very concerned
about their reputations. They don't want to look like they're being co-
opted," he says. While nonprofits do not object to accountability, if
they're delivering results, "cut us some slack about how the money is
spent."

Even though corporate giving programs are generally well-meaning in their intentions, the result can still backfire. Dana Serleff, president and CEO of the Every Child Can Learn Foundation, says the education-based nonprofit gets tons of proposals from companies that want to make education a centerpiece of their philanthropy. So, "out of a sense of corporate responsibility, they put together something that they want to deliver to schools," she says. The combination of all these efforts can be overwhelming and counterproductive. "Companies come at us as if we have infinite resources and they can just waste our time." For a hypothetical example, "What if every bank or financial institution created a financial literacy program and all of them wanted to deliver those to high schools?" Serleff notes. If there are 100 financial institutions all creating programs, how can the nonprofit community or the schools cope? "There are hundreds of good ideas that get dropped on schools by businesses, and then they wonder why we haven't incorporated them," she says. "We've got principals who are overseeing much bigger, consolidated schools. We're asking them to be academic leaders, business leaders, and integrators of everybody's charitable programs." She points out that, no matter how good the incoming advice is, schools have to integrate it with everything else they're supposed to do, including educating students. A school isn't set up to deal with a huge influx of suggestions, volunteers, or technology equipment. "When corporations get engaged in education, they don't just want to give their money. They want to get involved. If you get 10 partners and each of them wants to go in a different direction and send you 100 volunteers, school districts have a problem," Serleff says. Lately, a pet project has been to improve financial literacy in low-income communities by bringing projects into schools. She singles out Wells Fargo for praise, because instead of marching into the schools with its financial literacy tool, the banking company made the tool available on its Website to be used on an as-needed basis. That's the kind of help that schools appreciate, Serleff reports.

Christina Goodney, executive director of Young Audiences Silicon Valley, which tries to teach students about the arts, has had similar experiences to Serleff's. "A lot of corporate philanthropy is very focused on giving money to programs that offer specific services, like paying an artist to be in a classroom," she says. If every corporation has differing aims—one wants musicians, another visual artists, still another actors—it becomes very difficult for us, as nonprofits, to manage all the administrative aspects." Goodney would like to see "a greater understanding and support for what goes on behind the programs." Also, corporations often don't seem to realize that giving many small grants and expecting high accountability on all of them creates administrative nightmares. "The level of accountability goes up with the amount of the contribution," she says, something that corporations do not always appreciate. "If a company is making an investment, it's reasonable to expect the nonprofit will be run professionally and can keep track of where the money is spent and what programs are happening." But that doesn't mean that every corporation is going to get a quarterly accounting to the penny, Goodney says, especially if they're making $5,000 or $10,000 grants.

For these reasons, says Goodwin, of the Points of Light Foundation, it's increasingly important that companies concentrate their philanthropy and do it through meaningful partnerships with nonprofits. "What you want is an ongoing presence, as opposed to a hit-or-miss or episodic contribution," he says. Financing a project in "willy-nilly fashion, you may derive a temporary sense of gratification, but you won't be likely to replicate that experience, and you might have a disappointing experience the next time you go out." So he is a proponent of strategic philanthropy—tying social investment to areas "where you have the greatest amount of resources, skills, and assets." Goodwin believes strongly that this type of focused, in-depth effort will lead to long-term investment by corporate philanthropy, as opposed to the here-today-gone-tomorrow scattering of resources that frustrates both nonprofits and, ultimately, the donor too.

The Downright Ugly

If there's anything that nonprofits especially resent, it's corporate philanthropists who come barging in thinking that they know it all and can apply the organizational principles of the business world, unadulterated, to cleaning up the messy nonprofit world. This attitude was especially prevalent during the economic boom years of the later 1990s, when companies thought that applying their business and technological know-how could solve almost any problem. "There was this assumption that nonprofits were these country bumpkins who didn't know how to run a business," says SeniorNet's Wrixon. "They had the attitude: *I know better than you how money should be used because I have an MBA from Harvard.* I would be in these meetings where people who had done amazing things in the nonprofit community would be humiliated. Corporations would tell us that *you need to be more like us.* They would use business school terms rather than nonprofit terms." She adds that this arrogance has become far less prevalent today, although it still exists, but businesses have been humbled by the downturn in the economy and the scandals at companies such as Enron. Sums up Wrixon, "There has to be a mutual respect that you know your business, and they know theirs. You have to trust each other." That trust doesn't happen when one side figures it knows everything.

Another issue that makes nonprofits extremely leery of corporations is real or perceived conflict of interest. This can be especially tricky in an era of strategic philanthropy and "cause-related marketing," which combines traditional brand marketing with community service causes. The latter can work well if the boundaries are clear. For example, Cadence Design Systems' annual Stars & Strikes event raises hundreds of thousands of dollars for nonprofits and artfully enlists employee efforts. Dori Ives, a philanthropy and marketing consultant in Silicon Valley who has advised Cadence, says that company doesn't forget about the real impact of Stars & Strikes—which is not self-promotion, but aiding the community and giving employees and executives a bonding experience. "If you're doing [philanthropy] for the headlines or inches in the newspapers, you shouldn't be doing it," she says. "If you really don't understand what the community needs, but you assume you do, you shouldn't be doing it."

Share Our Strength, a Washington-based nonprofit that specializes in helping companies do cause-related marketing related to abolishing hunger and poverty, says it has to be cognizant of what the companies want as well as how that will look to outsiders. "There has to be a value proposition" for both sides, says Howard Byck, director of creative enterprises marketing for Share Our Strength. "We do promote brands, but we have to be cautious that we're not compromising our mission." For example, "we've taken a pass on tobacco money," which is problematic, even though those companies want to promote health and human services. Share Our Strength has also turned down a beer company because the promotion "was a little too risqué for us." On the other hand, the nonprofit often does events with spirit companies featuring wine and food tastings. "We address these case by case, partner by partner," says Byck. "We are not purists, but we are careful. You can find partnerships where you have shared values and the nature of the promotions is consistent with your mission."

Anyway, Byck adds, consumers "have become much more sophisticated and cynical about how companies are leveraging causes," and they will discount efforts that are blatantly self-promotional or hypocritical. Nonetheless, nonprofits need money, and "whether the money comes from a golf tournament or a wine tasting, it's still money for the system," Byck notes. He advises companies that such events should be integrated into an overall philanthropic program, not just set up as a reaction to a "cause du jour." Byck also encourages companies to look beyond the popular causes, such as education and breast cancer, to other areas of deep social need. That's why Share Our Strength is focused on fighting against poverty and hunger, causes which, at least in the United States, are "second-tier," he says. Of course corporations have to do philanthropy "that makes sense for them," but some important causes "tend to get lost." He asks corporations to be willing to peer beyond the obvious and find nonstandard ways to deliver community services. Otherwise, "anything that's not in that sweet spot runs the risk of being cut off from funding."

Hands Across the Profit Barrier

To a certain extent, there will always be an inequality between corporations and nonprofits. "Money talks," says Sterling Speirn, president of Peninsula Community Foundation in San Mateo, California. "You have to figure out what level of engagement or control [that corporations] want for their money." He adds that this attitude is nothing new. "Donors have always wanted to be cocreators of value and not just funders of value." That's fine, so long as donors are smart about what they do and work with the nonprofit to get smarter, he says. Shannon St. John, president of the Triangle Community Foundation, tries to think like companies in approaching them for grants. "I have very little patience with my fellow nonprofits who argue that they can't measure what they do," she says. "Part of what we do as a community foundation is to educate both corporate and individual donors about realistic expectations. Most nonprofits could use a healthy dose of that kind of discipline—like benchmarks. We also have to recognize that intractable human problems will not be solved overnight." An important part of philanthropy is the work that goes on behind the scenes; not the splashy project or event, but the day-to-day administration and accounting, evaluation, and feedback. These are not sexy, so they're neglected by many corporate philanthropists. "Philanthropy is not easy," says St. John. "It requires the same amount of concentration and expertise and administration as any other corporate activity."

The Good, the Bad, and the Ugly in Nonprofit/For-Profit Relationships

▸ **The good:** collaborative planning, patience, human resources to support cash, unrestricted funding that covers administrative costs, flexibility in scheduling projects.

▸ **The bad:** unrealistic objectives/timing, flooding of resources without determination of need, reliance on a single source of funds, overly strict reporting requirements.

▸ **The ugly:** Arrogance, using business acumen and processes without attempting to understand current processes and problems, focusing on self-promotion, blatant conflicts of interest.

The best way for corporate philanthropies to learn about the nonprofit world is to roll up their sleeves and get involved, suggests Jeff Sunshine, corporate services officer with Community Foundation Silicon Valley. "Then they get what it's all about. What's most startling for corporate folks is to see how under-resourced nonprofits are and how they have to patch things together to run their 'businesses.'" Again, this helps bridge the expectation gap that can occur when corporations expect overnight results. "Then there can be a little deflation," says Sunshine. "They think they're done when they're just getting started." Companies often underestimate the competence of nonprofit administrators, in part, because the monetary rewards are less than in the corporate world. But people go into nonprofit work for reasons other than money, and most executives in the field are highly skilled and dedicated. "You want to listen, not prescribe," Dinah Waldsmith, senior manager of Business for Social Responsibility, advises corporate philanthropists. "Be open to hearing what the reality is from the nonprofit's perspective, rather than creating an artificial separation between yourself as the funding source and them as the community organization."

The profit barrier can be breached. We've already given numerous examples of how that occurs in previous chapters, particularly the one on national partnerships (Chapter 11). Corporations and nonprofits each have too much to lose not to get along—and much to gain if they do. A business is only as strong as the community in which it's located. Tough social problems such as homelessness, crime, and poverty can only be tackled if the business and nonprofit worlds work together effectively. To do that, they need to appreciate each other's strengths and weaknesses, abilities and needs. "One essential is to have clearly articulated goals," says Christina Goodney, executive director of Young Audiences Silicon Valley. Nonprofits, with their long time frames, "need to be able to plan two or three years in advance," she says, so they want to make sure that their goals mesh with corporate goals. Not too many nonprofits are looking for quick handouts (except in emergencies); they prefer corporate partners who may start slow, but stick with them. Serleff adds that she likes partners to do their homework before approaching a nonprofit. "The hardest thing is the people who come at you as a nonprofit and say, 'I'm not sure what I want to do, but let's talk about it.'" For nonprofits, time is just as limited a resource as it is for corporate executives. The best corporate partners know what they're doing with philanthropy and why, can explain it to nonprofits and choose partners who meet their criteria, and then trust them to carry out the jointly agreed-upon goals.

Call to Alms—A Summary of the Top 10 Best Practices in Corporate Philanthropy

Like the astronauts who gazed upon this small, shimmering globe of ours—an island of life in the midst of the darkness of space—those who embrace corporate philanthropy realize that we're all in this together, and that companies cannot stand off to the side and pretend that they're separate from the world community. Timberland CEO Jeff Swartz gets it, decrying the "artificial demarcation between corporation and community." His own active service in Timberland projects, coupled with his observations of employees who participate, make him conscious of the fact that "the community is us," as he puts it, adding that, "it's imperative that all of us be engaged in building this community." Hasbro Chairman Alan Hassenfeld gets it too: "We believe in the motto, 'You make a living by what you do, you make a life by what you give.'" He urges companies that aren't involved in community service to get involved. "If a company wants to be part of the 21st century, it better understand what social responsibility means."

One of the assumptions of the Internet age is that location doesn't matter anymore. Maybe it doesn't in terms of ordering a product, but it certainly does in terms of community. "The ability to be highly productive and innovate quickly depends on location more than ever," asserts Mark Kramer, managing director of Foundation Strategy Group. "Companies' success is intertwined with the communities in which they operate. You cannot have a healthy community that doesn't have a sustainable economy. You cannot have a successful business in a dying community." The tragic events of 9/11 reminded us again that no nation, no matter how rich, can build walls that protect us from the suffering of the rest of the world. Similarly, no company can truly prosper for the long term if the community—and today that means the global community—isn't prospering along with it. We, as people privileged enough to live here in the United States and work for corporations whose revenues often dwarf those of entire countries, must do more to help others in ways that let them eventually help themselves. No one is suggesting that companies give back to the community out of pure altruism. Rather, it's because the very survival of a company lies in its interaction with the community that surrounds and nourishes it—providing employees, customers, and sustenance. "People have to realize that their success is built on the communities in which they're involved. Every successful company is successful because of the talent they're able to attract," says Levi Strauss CEO Phil Marineau. "We find that the values of the company and the notion of profits through principles is a key way of attracting people." He adds that the old conception "that business is only about business" doesn't apply anymore. "We need to make giving back a part of the mainstream and get people who are not part of this giving to join us."

An ethical framework that embraces community service can strengthen a company in good times and bad, winning it plaudits externally and imbuing leaders and employees with the understanding that they're part of something bigger than themselves. Doing philanthropy is an important component of being a good corporate citizen. Although a devotion to community service doesn't necessarily fend off scandals such as those that roiled Enron, WorldCom, and others, it's certainly a starting point toward an overall attitude that the bottom line isn't everything. The impact of a Timberland, a Hasbro, or a Levi Strauss reaches beyond the products they sell or the money they return to shareholders and owners. These companies stand for something. It's not always easy to define, but it's obvious to those who work for the companies or associate with them. And it's why consumers trust in their brands. One of the reasons that new executives came to Levi and employees stuck with it during a tough turnaround period is that "people want to be proud of where they work," says Marineau. "They're attracted by the values of the company. It's not just brand and reputation. It's about the quality of people you can attract to the company. We have sustained our giving and contributions in these times and the people we've attracted want to be associated with that."

If you've read this far in the book, you should be convinced by now of the value of philanthropy, so let's finish by summarizing the 10 "best practices" that make corporate community service do good and do well for the company and the community.

1. **Start developing a program today,** if you haven't already. No matter how small or strapped for resources you are, helping someone else will raise morale and make you feel like you're in charge of your destiny. "It doesn't relate to how much money you give away or how many employees you have," says Stan Litow, president of the IBM Foundation. If nothing else, inventory the skills of your employees and let them give of their time. Swartz puts it even more simply: "Just get into the game." If you don't think you have enough people to make a difference, invite others to join you. "Collaboration is a powerful model," he says. "We invite our suppliers to serve with us. We invite other companies. I believe small companies can be big companies by applying this model of leverage and engagement. It's an opportunity to access joy."

2. **Define a mission** by establishing priorities and make sure to communicate those to executives, employees, customers, nonprofit partners, and others. Have clear guidelines about what you do and don't fund, but enough flexibility to respond to emergencies. Don't make this communication blatantly self-promotional, because people will see through that. Dinah Waldsmith, senior manager for Business for Social Responsibility, advises companies to be open about their review process for grants and about their goals. "Help nonprofits to understand what you want from them," she says, "but don't create a process that's too burdensome."

3. **Integrate service with your corporate culture.** Make it a part of your "brand." Many companies have done this successfully, including Timberland, Levi Strauss, Hasbro, and LensCrafters. "Early on, we recognized the power we had to make a difference, and made a point of capturing and communicating these magic moments," says Susan Knobler, vice president of the LensCrafters Foundation, which runs the Gift of Sight program. Everyone at Lenscrafters can tell stories about someone who got glasses and saw their grandchild or the blackboard at school for the first time. "We developed a folklore that has become part of the company."

4. **Demonstrate commitment from the top down, and involve employees from the bottom up.** The best way for senior managers to show support for community service is by doing it themselves, as well as publicly championing its importance. "People will have a newfound appreciation for this work when they know the CEO and other executives give their own time and not just lip service," says Bob Goodwin, executive director of the Points of Light Foundation. He advises companies to develop written policies on flexible scheduling and released time to accommodate employee volunteerism. "Treat these in the same fashion as other benefits," he says, "as opposed to being seen as not worthy of the protocol of official procedures. This heightens visibility and credibility."

5. **Define your community broadly, in ways that make sense for the corporation.** Don't forget the rest of the world outside of North America, even though local customs and cultural barriers might make it more difficult to reach out. For LensCrafters, its community became anyone who needed glasses and couldn't get them. The Gift of Sight program overcomes challenges such as electrical outages, unfamiliar foods, equipment held up in customs, language differences, and less than ideal accommodations. "With experiences like this, who needs diversity training?" Knobler jokes.

6. **Forge strong partnerships with nonprofits and give them the respect you would any other business partner.** Corporations love to talk about leverage, and community service is an area ideally suited to it. Once you've identified your long-term vision of philanthropy, "use that to select nonprofits that will help you achieve that vision," advises Bill Shireman, CEO of the Global Futures Foundation. Look at how the nonprofit partners relate to each other and "make sure they're complementary and won't be competing with each other."

7. **Consider your business goals in developing your philanthropy, but don't be too rigid.** Treat philanthropy as an investment as important as any other. IBM and Hewlett-Packard, for example, have shown how investing in the community reaps value for the corporation in the form of patents, new customers, and positive media coverage. "Philanthropy must align the interests of the company and the community," says Shireman. "Once they're aligned, the more both can gain. It's a win-win situation." For example, a food products retailer

could help homeless shelters develop a distribution system. "You want to be as excited about philanthropy as your core business," he says. "It will give you strategic opportunities to increase your business." However, don't let this potential business opportunity color the underlying commitment to making the community a better place.

8. **Find ways to measure and to celebrate the impact of your philanthropy.** LensCrafters's stated goal was to help 3 million people through its Gift of Sight program by the end of 2003. "Gift of Sight has elevated our daily work and given us an energizing higher purpose," says Knobler. "We're not just selling glasses, we're changing lives." IBM's Litow suggests that companies should not only set measurable goals with their nonprofit partners, they should also "benchmark themselves against other companies that are doing this well." In the business world, he notes, "people are savagely trying to steal and borrow business processes across companies. Do the same thing with philanthropy. Find the best practices and learn how to make them work for you."

9. **Sustain your philanthropy even when the company is going through tough times.** Responsible companies that plan to be around for a long time should pace their philanthropy inversely to the marketplace, advises Shireman. That is, they should maximize their philanthropic efforts during economic downturns. "You're going to be helping people who will remember your help," he says. "Philanthropic givers will be more appreciated for providing for these needs when they're acute." You may need to reduce cash giving during a financial slowdown, on par with other departmental cuts, so giving more of your time or product to offset this is critical. The worst thing you can do during a layoff period is to reduce service programs, because that will further diminish morale of the remaining employees. Doing volunteer projects is one of the best ways to put things into perspective and increase the cohesiveness of a team.

10. **Don't be afraid to change or to try new things.** After all, your core business has had to adapt to the Internet era, globalization, and instant communication, why not your philanthropy? The ability to dig deeper into what the community needs and confront how you have not yet been addressing that is key in building future programs that will be high-impact. You need to continually tweak and improve philanthropic programs, to ensure that they are as impactful as they can be. Litow says

the revolution going on in technology—providing products and services on an as-needed basis—should also apply to philanthropy. "We've got to move to on-demand community service," he says. Innovative community service becomes an important differentiator for companies, one that they'll hesitate to cut—even in difficult times.

(🌍) . . . .

Corporate Giving Options

▸ **Corporate foundation:** A separate, legal foundation that gets its grant-making funds primarily from the corporation itself, either in the form of an endowment (stock) or pass-through funds donated each year.

▸ **Corporate giving program:** A grant-making program established and administered within a profit-making company. The program's budget is part of the company's overall budgeting process.

▸ **Community foundations (see Chapter 12):** A publicly supported nonprofit intermediary that collects and disburses funds from multiple donors, including individuals and corporations.

▸ **In-kind donations:** Donations of equipment, supplies, and other materials for use by nonprofits. The donor may be able to take a tax incentive for up to twice the product cost for inventory contributed to nonprofits.

▸ **Employee volunteerism and matching gifts:** Companies coordinate and encourage employee volunteerism through various mechanisms, including paid time off. They also may match employee donations to nonprofits with corporate funds.

▸ **Cause-related marketing:** A commercial activity sponsored by a company that markets a particular event or product, such as a sports contest, to produce a marketing benefit. Proceeds of the event are donated to nonprofits.

. . . . (🌍)

We quoted Martin Luther King, Jr. at the start of this book. The comment bears repeating, "Everyone can be great because everyone can serve." Philanthropy is the currency that sustains the social contract and bridges the chasms that divide us. An individual or a company that does not connect with the community is isolated from one of the most meaningful, important, *human* callings: the need to serve. LensCrafter's Knobler calls serving the community a "virtuous cycle" that reinforces corporate culture and promotes bonding between employees, executives, and people in the community. At salesforce.com, philanthropy has played a key role in our success—attracting dedicated employees, giving them a balance to their lives, providing a connection point for global unity, and helping us win customers and partners. The Foundation is the secret weapon that keeps us grounded. People are here to do more than just make money. The company would be a very different, far bleaker place without our philanthropic mission. Because we're giving, we're able to receive. From those to whom much is given, much is expected back.

Endnotes

Chapter 5

1. University of Southern California *Networker*, Volume 8, Number 2, Interview with Carol Bartz, November/December 1997.

Chapter 7

1. Kanter, Rosabeth Moss, "From Spare Change to Real Change: The Social Sector as Beta Site for Business Innovation," *Harvard Business Review*, May-June 1999.

2. Ibid.

3. Boudreau, John, "Cisco 'Fellows' Spread Goodwill," *San Jose Mercury News*, February 14, 2003, posted on *www.bayarea.com*.

Chapter 9

1. Porter, Michael E., and Mark R. Kramer, "The Competitive Advantage of Corporate Philanthropy," *Harvard Business Review*, December 2002.

2. Ibid.

3. Packard, David, *The HP Way: How Bill Hewlett and I Built Our Company*, HarperBusiness, 1995, p. 166.

Chapter 10

1. Dunn, Debra, and Keith Yamashita, "Microcapitalism and the Megacorporation," *Harvard Business Review*, August 2003, pp. 46–54.

Chapter 13

1. World Economic Forum, "Philanthropy Measures Up," January 2003, p. 50.

2. The Center for Corporate Citizenship at Boston College, "Measurement Demystified: Determining the Value of Corporate Community Involvement," 2001, p. 35.

3. Ibid, p. 34.

Index

About the Authors

Marc Benioff is CEO and chairman of salesforce.com, a leading provider of online business applications, and creator of the salesforce.com Foundation. A former sales and marketing executive at Oracle Corporation, he is now enlisting his energy and ambition in building a new model for global philanthropy, as portrayed in this book.

Karen Southwick is an experienced journalist who has worked for several magazines, including *Forbes ASAP* and *Upside*, and metropolitan daily newspapers, including the *San Francisco Chronicle*. She has written four books on the business side of technology, most recently *Everyone Else Must Fail: The Unvarnished Truth about Oracle and Larry Ellison*, published in November 2003 by Random House/Crown. She is currently an executive editor at CNET News.com.